THEATRE SYM
A PUBLICATION OF THE SOUTHEASTERN

Cross-Cultural Dialogue
on the Global Stage

Volume 25

Published by the

Southeastern Theatre Conference and

The University of Alabama Press

THEATRE SYMPOSIUM is published annually by the Southeastern Theatre Conference, Inc. (SETC), and by the University of Alabama Press. SETC nonstudent members receive the journal as a part of their membership under rules determined by SETC. For information on membership, write to SETC, 1175 Revolution Mill Drive, Studio 14, Greensboro, NC 27405. All other inquiries regarding subscriptions, circulation, purchase of individual copies, and requests to reprint materials should be addressed to The University of Alabama Press, Box 870380, Tuscaloosa, AL 35487-0380.

THEATRE SYMPOSIUM publishes works of scholarship resulting from a single-topic meeting held on a southeastern university campus each spring. A call for papers to be presented at that meeting is widely publicized each autumn for the following spring. Authors are encouraged to send unsolicited manuscripts directly to the editor. Information about the next symposium is available from the incoming editor, Sarah McCarroll, Department of Communication Arts, 1332 Southern Drive, Statesboro, GA 30458, smccarroll @ georgiasouthern.edu.

THEATRE SYMPOSIUM
A PUBLICATION OF THE SOUTHEASTERN THEATRE CONFERENCE

Volume 25   *Contents*   *2017*

Introduction

Becky K. Becker

Globalization is nothing new. We need only look to the ancient Silk Road linking the Far East to the Mediterranean in order to find some of the earliest recorded impacts of people and goods crossing borders. Yet in the current cultural moment, tensions are high due to increased migration, economic unpredictability, complicated acts of local and global terror, and heightened political divisions all over the world. Because it is the moment in which we are living, it is all too easy to perceive globalization as "new" and therefore a threat to our ways of life, to our nations, and to our cultures. Britain's unexpected vote to leave the European Union in June 2016 is just one indicator—albeit a stunning one—of the degree to which individuals, communities, and nation-states are concerned about the impacts of border crossings, cross-cultural relationships, and the global economy.

The current response to globalization is nothing new either. Like the ebb and flow of time, our awareness, understanding, and valuing of cross-cultural relationships fluctuate according to the cultural climate in which they are shaped. For example, if we look at the lead-up to World War I in Europe, many of the tensions we are currently experiencing may feel like echoes of that time. Similarly, a bit closer to home, the rhetoric of the 2016 presidential election, and unexpected win for Donald Trump, is reminiscent of previous populist campaigns and, more specifically, the cultural climate in the United States in 1968, with all its divisiveness and volatility. Despite decades of perceived growth and change, ostensibly impacted by such historical markers as the civil rights movement, the women's movement, the Vietnam War, the Korean War, the Gulf War, 9/11, and subsequent crises in the Middle East that are ongoing, we find ourselves in a time of increased division and skepticism toward migrants and refugees, global economic and political relationships, and our ability to find solutions to both international and domestic problems.

Contributing to this divide is the increased rate at which information is dispersed. While it means that we can be informed more quickly of significant events and movements across the world, there is also a risk of media saturation, false information, and our immediate ability to share knee-jerk responses to complex social and cultural issues that cannot be meaning-fully communicated in 140 characters or less. For example, accusations have been directed toward Black Lives Matter here in the United States for being too politically correct in their responses to the "All Lives Mat-ter" counter-campaign. Yet, rather than perceiving Black Lives Matter as a necessary response to police violence and high incarceration rates that specifically target people of color in the United States, "All Lives Matter" works as a means to minimize the lived experiences of African Americans and oversimplify or dilute the dialogue. The perceived political correct-ness that emerged during the US cultural and identity revolution of the 1990s is passed off as being weak and unfair rather than acknowledging its original intent: increased cultural sensitivity and thoughtful dialogue.

Cultural moments such as this one are a stark reminder that for some, empathetic and sensitive communication unnecessarily detracts from the power of the dominant culture. Perhaps even more disturbing, it seems to be a strategy to curtail cross-cultural dialogue that acknowledges com-plexity. When right-wing politicians characterize all refugees and migrants as potential terrorists, denigrating their liberal counterparts for refusing to use the term "radical Islamic terrorist," the strategy is to deny complexity and, more poignantly, to portray such attempts at cultural sensitivity as being "weak on terror." In one fell swoop a serious global issue—in-creased migration due to civil unrest, ongoing wars, dwindling resources, climate change, and, in some instances, terrorism—impacting millions of innocent people, is reduced to its most politically charged component. Cultural sensitivity, by association, is perceived to be a bad idea, signify-ing weakness. Meaningful cross-cultural dialogue that is sensitive to our shared histories, cultures, and perceived differences is reduced to pander-ing by those who would make a mockery of it. Dialogue becomes impos-sible. Saying anything becomes too great a risk.

At a time when cross-cultural dialogue within our own country and among countries across the globe feels strained—even threatened—what is the role of theatre? How do we fit within the ongoing development of meaningful cross-cultural dialogue and social change? How has theatre been impacted by globalization and humanity's increasing need to under-stand the world as an intricately connected community? In what ways have theatre practitioners, educators, and scholars worked to support cross-cul-tural dialogue historically? And in what ways might we work to support ongoing dialogue that embraces the complexities and contradictions in-herent to any meaningful exchange?

Cross-cultural dialogue in theatre is nothing new. From ancient Egypt, India, and Greece, whose theatrical practices were influenced by the intermingling of cultures, to the early modernists, whose influences tended to be indigenous peoples from South America, Africa, and Southeast Asia, theatre has contributed to ongoing cross-cultural exchange. Even when such cultural transactions have gone mostly unacknowledged, the impact of the exchange remains. As an example, Egypt's cultural influence on ancient Greece—perceived to be the birthplace of Western theatre—has until recently been overlooked, perpetuating the assumption that the classical world sprang solely from its own inherent richness. Since the mid-twentieth century practitioners such as Bertolt Brecht, Peter Brook, and Jerzy Grotowski have purposefully engaged other cultures to bring innovative staging and themes to light. More recently, US practitioners Anna Deavere Smith, Robbie McCauley, and Lin-Manuel Miranda, among others, have made cross-cultural dialogue central to their dramaturgy, serving to illuminate a variety of cultural backgrounds while contributing to a complex depiction of the global community.

Given our increasingly globalized world and the blurring of nation and identity as borders shift and cultures mingle, cross-cultural dialogue would seem to be the new normal for contemporary theatre. Yet in many locations across the United States, theatre seasons have remained relatively Eurocentric, likely a reflection of the wider entertainment world in which TV and film often struggle to incorporate diverse perspectives—when they even bother trying. Despite some theatre practitioners' hesitance to respond to increasing globalization and cultural changes closer to home, there are examples, both historical and contemporary, of theatre artists working to contribute to the wide array of cross-cultural dialogue in all its complexity. In what ways, then, have theatre practitioners and scholars responded to rapid globalization? What are significant examples of cross-cultural dialogue that have gone unnoticed, historically? What have we learned from our counterparts across the globe? And what constitutes dialogue that goes beyond innovative practice to engage theatre practitioners and audience members in transforming our global awareness in meaningful ways? These and many other questions were considered as thirty theatre scholars/practitioners gathered for Theatre Symposium 25, April 22–24, 2016, on the campus of Agnes Scott College in Decatur, Georgia.

Contributing to discussion throughout the symposium was keynote speaker Anita Gonzalez, Professor of Theatre and Drama and head of the Global Theatre and Ethnic Studies minor at the University of Michigan. In her keynote address, "Theatre as Cultural Exchange: Stages and Studios of Learning," Gonzalez laid the groundwork for discussions revolving around cross-cultural collaboration, ways of embodying culture, cultural exchange versus unauthorized cultural borrowing, the centrality of empathy to any intercultural endeavor, and the important role educators, practitioners, and scholars play in supporting cross-cultural dialogue. As the weekend progressed, the overarching theme, that meaningful cross-cultural dialogue must be intentional, was underscored by the many ways in which theatre practitioners and scholars engage in and understand intercultural theatre and its influences.

Throughout the weekend, papers ranged from traditional historical research of specific cultural groups and their influences on Western theatre to contemporary depictions of culture—including race, ethnicity, gender, and sexuality. Urmila Palit asked audience members to consider potential influences of ancient Bengali theatre on its Western counterpart, ancient Greek theatre, while Seth Wilson advocated that Aphra Behn presented a sympathetic portrayal of indigenous peoples in her play *The Widow Ranter* in seventeenth-century England. Focusing on Eastern influences on the West, Michele Dormaier examined Orientalist depictions of the Middle East in Western ballet, while Tony Gunn looked at Edward Gorey's use of Japanese and Chinese design motifs in interpreting Western productions. Exploring cross-cultural dialogue within Western culture, Lawrence Smith considered French existentialist influences on Ingmar Berman's films. In addition to these and other historical examinations, a number of papers concentrated on cross-cultural collaboration as a meaningful though often complicated process. To that end, Josh Kelly analyzed Peter Brook's quest for universals along with successes and failures at cultural sensitivity in *Conference of the Birds*; John Grote provided a fascinating description of Americans adapting Shakespeare's *A Midsummer Night's Dream* with Vietnamese actors and the significance of mutual respect in such collaborations; and Sarah McCarroll evaluated unintended echoes of imperialism in the Globe Theatre's "Globe to Globe" Festival of 2012, which coincided with the London Olympic Games. Providing philosophical observations of contemporary plays and playwrights, Geoffrey Douglas examined cross-cultural representations in the play *Take Me Out*, while Tia Ade-Salu analyzed different approaches to spirituality in multi-generation and first-generation African American playwrights. Finally, lending complexity to the current national focus on violence on the Mexican border, Sonora Ann Ruelas described a documentary-style theatre production giving voice to citizens in the Rio Grande Valley.

As the range and diversity of papers from Theatre Symposium 25 suggest, cross-cultural dialogue tends to be messy. Far from being a straightforward, formulaic, predictable process, the kind of collaboration and dialogue required for meaningful exchange is tricky—at times frustrating, bumpy, and temperamental; at other times exhilarating, joyful, and fun. Here, I am reminded of a recent study abroad experience leading a group of student performers in Kiryu, Japan. Central to the program was a cross-cultural exchange with an all-male local dance group in Kiryu who agreed to teach us the art of Kagura, a nonverbal, physically precise, masked performance form and precursor to Noh theatre. As exciting as this exchange was, it also posed a number of challenges. A short rehearsal process meant that we had one intensive week to learn and prepare a program for the city's mayor and other local elites; none of us spoke Japanese, our teachers spoke little English, and the few interpreters we had were scheduled sporadically during our rehearsal process; gender, age, and racial differences between the all-male, middle-aged Japanese Kagura group and our group of three males and eleven females, including six African Americans and three middle-aged professors, posed other discrete challenges to the cross-cultural communication process; finally, the Stanislavski-based background of the American performers (of which I was one, along with all of my students) meant that we were not accustomed to learning by repeating the actions of the master teacher. As might be expected, the path toward understanding was not smooth. The American performers struggled to learn a new performance style and method, while the Japanese teachers maneuvered to adapt to students whose lack of Japanese language skills only added to the challenge. Yet somehow at the end of a chaotic, invigorating, and generative process, we found ourselves performing in front of our Japanese sister-city audience, feeling proud and grateful for the experience. Perhaps most importantly, despite our inability to communicate through spoken word, a meaningful cross-cultural dialogue was cultivated through gesture, translation, intuition, and laughter.

In keeping with the expansive description of cross-cultural dialogue fostered by paper presentations and discussions throughout the symposium, this volume represents a range of strategies and perspectives. In an expanded version of her keynote presentation, "Theatre as Cultural Exchange: Stages and Studios of Learning," Anita Gonzalez encourages readers to embrace collaboration, exchange, and finding the global in the local as the means for practitioners, educators, and scholars to bring depth to our cross-cultural collaborations. E. Bert Wallace describes a cross-cultural research process prompted by a small, misquoted historical passage in "Certain Kinds of Dances Used among Them: An Initial Inquiry into Colonial Spanish Encounters with the *Areytos* of the *Taíno* in Puerto Rico." His essay sheds light on the unexpected journeys scholarly inquiry often requires. Sunny Stalter-Pace and Chase Bringardner examine historical moments of cultural appropriation in "Gertrude Hoffmann's Lawful Piracy: 'A Vision of Salome' and the Russian Season as Transatlantic Production Impersonations" and "Greasing the Global: Princess Lotus Blossom and the Fabrication of the 'Orient' to Pitch Products in the American

Medicine Show," respectively. Both essays grapple with problematic historical figures whose performance work can be instructive when considered more carefully in context. In "Dismembering Tennessee Williams: The Global Context of Lee Breuer's *A Streetcar Named Desire*," Daniel Ciba discusses the 2011 Comédie Française production in which, he argues, Breuer worked to disengage Williams's well-known play from its iconic American productions, presenting a less localized and more globalized interpretation. Karen Berman recounts her experiences directing Georgia students in original plays abroad in "Transformative Cross-Cultural Dialogue in Prague: Americans Creating Czech History Plays." Describing their own theatrical processes abroad, Erica Tobolski and Deborah A. Kinghorn discuss the importance of cultural knowledge and the actor's first language to cross-cultural voice training in "Finding Common Ground: Lessac Training across Cultures." Mirroring the diverse range of possibilities cross-cultural dialogue in theatre represents, these essays provide a rich array of descriptions, experiences, and processes that contribute to its complexity.

Cross-cultural dialogue is an arduous endeavor—at once delicate, complicated, uncomfortable, exciting, and fun. Thankfully, due to the generosity of many individuals, the symposium and, for that matter, this journal have involved relatively smooth collaborations. This year's keynoter and respondent, Anita Gonzalez, offered a warm and collegial manner, delivering informative insights into her own cross-cultural work and inspiring symposium participants to seek out new ways of engaging in global and local exchange. As is his usual manner, past editor and host David S. Thompson, the Annie Louise Harrison Waterman Professor of Theatre at Agnes Scott College, provided valuable logistical support and a good dose of humor as preparations were made for the symposium. For the second year in a row, Agnes Scott Faculty Administrative Assistant Leah Owenby worked the registration table while I attended to other responsibilities, contributing to a calm, relaxed beginning to the symposium. Theatre Symposium is known by return participants to be an open, unpretentious venue for rich conversations and connections. This is due, in no small part, to the Theatre Symposium Steering Committee comprising J. K. Curry, Philip G. Hill, Scott Phillips, David S. Thompson, and Bert Wallace; I am grateful to each of them for their generosity and guidance. This volume would not be possible without the careful work of the Theatre Symposium editorial board; I cannot thank them enough for their work reviewing submissions and providing insightful commentary. Thanks also to Betsey Horth and the entire staff at the SETC central office, as well as to Daniel Waterman and the editorial staff of the University of Alabama Press, who make what may seem like an insurmountable task very straightforward and manageable. Associate editor Sarah McCarroll has been a truly invaluable partner. Thank you, Sarah, for your discerning eye and your delightful sense of humor, both of which have been indispensable. As ever, to my husband, Mark Jarzewiak: thank you for understanding my need to travel, for traveling with me much of the time, and for supporting my journeys when you cannot. Thank you, most of all, for being the culturally curious and empathetic person you are. I cannot imagine making the journey without you.

Theatre as Cultural Exchange

Stages and Studios of Learning

Anita Gonzalez

It was a pleasure presenting for "Theatre Symposium: Cross-Cultural Dialogue on the Global Stage" in April 2016. The symposium offered a unique opportunity to dialogue with colleagues about how global perspectives influence our practice. Whether we work in performance, technical production, or theatre studies, our artistry and scholarship expand when we take time to learn about other cultures and consider how our production seasons, classrooms, and professional work might change by introducing world perspectives. Global travel begins in our minds. We must first imagine a broad context for what we consider to be theatre; then we can engage with new paradigms that will define the future of our artistic forms. Even though we work in diverse contexts, each of our areas of expertise can benefit from engaging with literature and practices that take us away from our comfort zones. Intercultural experiences, coupled with meaningful interactions with people who differ from us, expand our minds. As the head of the Global Theatre and Ethnic Studies minor at the University of Michigan in Ann Arbor, I advocate for theatre practices that foreground diverse cultures and promote engagement with intercultural communities. "Going global" enhances our ability to absorb multiple perspectives that can broaden our understandings about theatrical practice.

Often I hear that we are all humans under the skin, but through my travels and classroom experiences I have learned that while we share common emotions and physiques, ideologies and belief systems can be really different. And that is the beautiful thing about the theatre. It provides an opportunity to physically, viscerally experience another perspective of human existence. As a scholar and practitioner I find performance to be an ideal way of crossing borders. When I think about stages and studios of learning I wonder, how do we teach for a global future? Most theatre programs offer a combination of literature and studio courses coupled with a production season. In general, we remain committed to teaching a canon of plays that reflect the history of Euro-American, English-language theatre. Global and multicultural theatre appears as the spice to enrich our experience of a progressive historical evolution of Western drama.

Escaping this approach to theatrical training is a challenge because, as faculty members, often this has been our training, our experience, or our area of expertise. It is intimidating to approach learning about the cultures of the entire world. In addition to a plethora of plays, there are language barriers. And if each cultural drama represents a distinct ideology and cultural context, then how can we immerse ourselves in all of these deep histories and experiences?

We can begin to connect to other cultural positions just by considering our own background and heritage. Each of us brings experiences gleaned from a lifetime of immersion in a unique cultural context. Too often, we underestimate the impact of our learned cultural behaviors on our daily arts practice. Faculty members and students in American classrooms tend to think of themselves as part of an assimilated, hegemonic middle class. If we consider our ancestral heritage, each of us actually carries distinct cultural knowledges or understandings. For example, we tend to forget that our grandparents may have come from Ireland or that we might have been raised on a farm or an island rather than within a suburban community. Our heritage connections travel across generations and impact our worldview.[1]

One of the exercises I introduce in class to help students begin to think about global identities is to have them "perform their identity" as an opening activity. When I start this exercise, at first there is confusion. White students tell me they do not know what to perform. African American students ask me if they can perform any identity. I encourage all students to select a song, dance, or poem that is about who they are and to perform it. Within this exercise I have seen poignant theatrical acts. One performance that stands out for me is the work of a student of Swedish descent who performed a ritual of stuffing Christmas sausages. He stood in front of the class and began to demonstrate how to grind and stuff the meat. Then he spoke about his brother joining him in filling the casings, and as he worked he recalled how this activity connected him with family and heritage. He cried while performing this memory, remembering an almost-forgotten ethnic heritage. This performance of identity is just one of many that students have presented that point to our global environment. What is interesting about doing this exercise over time is the vast regional differences that emerge from the same assignment.

In New York, students tend to perform hyphenated identities—Italian

American, Irish American, Jewish American. In Florida, people performed geographic locales—being northern redneck or being from Miami or Georgia. When I teach in Michigan today, students often perform Detroit, a city—and for the first time last semester I observed students performing their identities as test-tube babies. The world is changing and it is hard to keep up. There are real challenges in thinking about how to relate theatre training to all of these identities. How do we incorporate a globalized world into our research and theatre-training programs? I propose we think about three modes of bringing global consciousness to theatre: collaboration, exchange, and finding the global in the local.

Collaboration

Since each of us is most familiar with our own cultural contexts, it is easiest to learn about other cultures through collaboration. Working with someone from a different background allows both partners to experience new ideas. In collaborations, we tend to carry a lot of unexamined assumptions with us. Studies document first-world or upper-middle-class tendencies to approach cultural exchange with a "savior" mentality. This means that we enter any cultural exchange believing that our own experiences, when shared, will enhance and improve the culture we are visiting. Inherent in this approach is an assumption that our partnering cultural community needs or wants to be assimilated into our behavioral modes. Even when we try to accommodate other cultural modes, we can lose sight of our own myopic visions.

Here is an example from graduate school. When I was working on my PhD at the University of Wisconsin–Madison, I was charged with directing a play called *El Guitarron* by Lynn Alvarez in collaboration with the university's Latino students. For this production, the department made a strong effort to recruit and involve Latino students. It was assumed that theatre students would contribute knowledge of theatre practice while the Latinos would contribute cultural knowledge to make the show a success.

Yet hidden in this plan were a lot of assumptions about *how* theatre should be done. We presumed that time would work the same across cultures, with everyone showing up ten minutes before rehearsals ready to work. That didn't happen. We presumed that our priorities would be the same and that the play's needs would take precedence over other activities, like family gatherings. That didn't happen. Things really came to a head when we presumed that Latino audiences would adjust to our theatrical ticket-buying rituals—that people who wanted to see the show would come to the box office to buy tickets. Our Latino collaborators told us that in their community, people sell tickets by holding a block of tickets, selling off individual tickets to family and friends, and then returning the unsold tickets and the money to the sponsor. The department was unable to accommodate this procedure, so we ended up with primarily university audience members.

My point here is that a successful collaboration needs dialogue and discussion. At the University of Wisconsin, and in many institutions, it is assumed that non-institutional communities will assimilate and adapt to the institution's norms. This creates an unbalanced circumstance in which the non-institutional is devalued. Offering a collaborative opportunity ideally means that both sides are willing and able to make adjustments. The Latino students' approach to selling tickets to the production was not incorrect or in need of improvement; it was merely a different solution to the play's outreach and promotion needs.

Currently, I am involved in another theatre project called the Storytelling Incubator, a collaboration with the Sault Ste. Marie Chippewa Tribe.[2] When I moved to Michigan to form the Global Theatre and Ethnic Studies minor, I immediately looked for local partners. I was introduced to the Upper Peninsula and the Chippewa community of Michigan through Dana Sitzler, a colleague from our Government Relations office. Our exchange activities with the Sault Ste. Marie community have taken about a year to develop and we are still exploring the twists and turns. As I began the process of working in this very rural community, I understood that notions of what theatre is might be distinct.

We began by meeting with two sectors of the community, historians from the town and members of the Chippewa tribe's cultural education department. Each had a very different idea about the purpose of our project and about how the town's history might be told. After discussions, we decided to first immerse our students in teachings about Anishinabek Chippewa traditions, and then to develop a workshop and performance program that might unite both sectors of the community in common activities. During the first part of the project, students stayed at the Mary Murray Culture Camp on Sugar Island, where they participated in sunrise ceremonies and teachings about corn and fire.[3] They were able to meet and share stories with both elders and youth of the community. In the process, they learned about themselves and came to question the way they were educated in their school programs about Native American presence in the United States. The experience of cultural exchange allowed students to think about who they were and what they knew from a different perspective. In the process, they gained self-awareness about their own cultural beliefs.

The second part of the Storytelling Incubator expanded our collaboration to include the town as well as the tribal community. While our

Figure 1. Students participating in the Storytelling Incubator project remove kernels from hard Indian corn as they learn how to prepare corn soup. The Sault Ste. Marie Chippewa Tribe education department invited elders to teach the university students cultural traditions as part of the theatre exchange project. Photograph by Anita Gonzalez.

goal was to unite the two communities, in practice we worked separately with two organizations: the Soo Theatre and the Chippewa Tribe. We found that these two cultural institutions operated within very different aesthetic traditions. Ultimately the project was best served by organizing distinct exchange activities. The main objective of our second phase was to present a staged reading of a play about domestic violence, *Sliver of a Full Moon*, by Oklahoma Cherokee Nation author Mary Katherine Nagle.[4] We were able to utilize tribal facilities for housing students and for rehearsals. For the performances, tribal administrators also gave us access to The Dream Catchers Theatre, a state-of-the art facility located within the Kewadin Casino complex. The space offers lights, catering services, and a stage with a dance floor.

Cultural differences in this collaboration emerged once again around production mechanisms. Because the play directly addresses sensitive issues of violence against women, our partners suggested we consult with three local organizations: the Chippewa Advocacy Resource Center, the Diane Peppler Center, and Uniting Three Fires against Violence, a statewide advocacy organization. In this collaboration, we did not want to make decisions without considering tribal perspectives about how a public event should be handled. We incorporated honoring and healing songs into the presentation because the Native American community wanted to honor the women for their bravery in telling their stories. The healing songs provided support and helped to ease any emotional trauma the women might have felt as they relived their traumatic experiences. Throughout the process we adapted our theatrical practice to accommodate an alternative approach to storytelling through performance that would heal the community by making public the stories of women who had been harmed by violence.

Figure 2. University of Michigan student Mia Massimino listens as a docent explains settler history of the Sault Ste. Marie region during a tour of one of the historic houses. An engaged learning exchange project educated students about history and culture of European settlers and Native Americans in this Canadian border town. Photograph by John R. Diehl Jr.

Outside of the reservation, we conducted workshops with community members. Students and faculty members interacted with the Soo Theatre, the town's European cultural community theatre, by offering workshops in theatre games as well as musical theatre and opera practice. Collen Arbic, president of the Soo Theatre, supported our residency by introducing us to her theatre's membership. We held informational meetings with local, nontribal theatre practitioners, but they did not participate in production activities for staging the Native American play.

Each community, even within the same town, approached the business of theatre-making differently. Ultimately I do not know that we were able to bridge cultural differences across the two Sault Ste. Marie communities. Even though some of the tribal facilities were directly across the street from the local Soo Theatre, it was hard to bring the two constituencies, the white European descendant community and the Native American community, into the same space. One group was invested in the Eurocentric arts of opera and ballet, while the other valued Native American cultural events such as powwows and bingo. Our performance brought a few members of the non-native community into the Kewadin casino performance space, but most of our audience members were also tribal members. Nevertheless, by collaborating on a project that crossed cultural lines, students were able to experience how different processes of performance can be. They could see the limits of collaboration, and we all learned that sometimes bridges cannot be realized.

International Exchange

International exchange, like any collaboration, brings artists together to swap ideas. Most international exchange programs emphasize summer- or semester-long study at a foreign university. Some schools offer faculty-led programs. For American theatre folk, the most common destination is London. While I have led programs in Mexico and Costa Rica, I am going to focus on four different UK projects because each project engaged with British culture differently. Some involved observation and tourist experiences, while others immersed students in one-on-one dialogic exchange with local partners.

It seems natural to travel to England to study theatre because the language is the same as in the United States and we have heard so much about Shakespeare. We want to immerse our students in the history and culture of the Bard. Still, I would like to point out that there are many other global sites for English-language theatre—Nigeria, the Caribbean, South Africa, Toronto—but here I will focus on England, describing four international exchange programs that I have led. My first UK project was simply attending plays. The State University of New York at New Paltz has an annual program where students spend two weeks seeing about ten plays in London. The program introduces students to styles of British professional theatre and allows them to experience such historical London sites as the reconstructed Globe Theatre. With this program, I most appreciated the way that the students' eyes lit up as they discovered life in a country where theatre has been supported and nurtured for centuries. Because my students at that time were New Yorkers, they were less impressed with the vibrancy of the city and more impressed with the multiple aesthetics and culturally diverse plays they were able to see in London.

Figure 3. University students from Michigan sit on a mountaintop outside of Oaxaca, Mexico. One among many study abroad offerings led by Anita Gonzalez, the international exchange program took students out of their comfort zones and exposed them to new ways of thinking about art and culture. Photograph by Omar Alonso.

After two years of leading this type of excursion, I proposed a more immersive experience in which students would be able to devise new work and learn with British practitioners. For this second, three-week experience, the students were housed at Kingston University. In addition to classes in British culture, they also participated in six workshops with British artists—producers, scholars, choreographers, directors—to learn how they might develop new work within the British landscape. The workshops increased student immersion in cross-cultural dialogue.

After completing the workshops, the class participated in a devising project, which involved reimagining scenes from *The Tempest* while thinking about gender-specific and postcolonial responses to the play. While
the students could have studied the play at home in their classrooms and
learned about Caliban as a postcolonial subject, or about how the opening shipwreck scene connects with the history of Jamestown, the project allowed the students to connect with local artists. They learned more
about British perspectives on the play and made professional connections
with British directors and scholars.

My third UK exchange was supported by the Global Intercultural
Experience for Undergraduates (GIEU) program at the University of
Michigan. This exchange program offered an opportunity to travel with
students to Liverpool and engage with the black communities of this
northern port town.[5] We spent one month interacting with local partners
and arts organizations. After learning about Liverpool, students worked in
small teams to volunteer with local not-for-profit agencies, including Africa Oye, The Brouhaha Carnival, The Green House Project, The Somali
Women's Project, and the Black E performance space. Our coordinating
community partner and sponsoring agency was the Merseyside Dance Initiative (MDI).[6] In addition to helping us to connect with the agencies,
MDI arranged housing and located a theatre for us to perform in. Because
the students collaborated closely with local artists, they were able to really
see differences and similarities between British and American cultures.

The students learned about black identity and how it works differently
on the other side of the water. For example, African American female students noticed that white British men found them attractive and compli-
mented them, something that seldom happened in their hometown of
Detroit. They also recognized that US historical events, such as the civil
rights movement and the life and death of Dr. Martin Luther King Jr. had
limited impact on the British community. Most of all, the student trav-
elers learned about themselves. When British people asked the American
students where they were from, most could offer no response other than
the name of their hometowns. Recognizing this lack of heritage, the students began to reconsider their identities and how to describe their point
of origin. At the end of the project we developed and performed a devised show for our community partners.[7] The play incorporated student
perspectives about their experiences and allowed them to verbalize their
feelings about their identities and those of their British collaborators. In
one section of the play, they performed what surprised them about British customs: tea, small cars, politeness, and language differences. Later
in the play, they talked about their newly gained understandings of class,
their concerns about social justice, and the challenges that America offers

for social mobility. This project was particularly satisfying because it was both educational and community-based, allowing students to use theatre to learn about another culture through engaged and interactive activities.

The current UK project I am working on has allowed students to collaborate as performers in a professional international theatrical production. Building upon my own academic research about African American transatlantic voyaging, I am collaboratively writing a new musical called *Liverpool Trading* with the black British composer Errollyn Wallen.[8] The project has been developed in both New York City and Liverpool, and each stage of the process has tested me as an artist and administrator. The story follows an Afro-Caribbean woman named Ayanna, who goes to Liverpool in search of her father. After she lands, an Irish pub owner named Monroe leads her on a time-traveling journey. As Ayanna searches for her ancestors, she discovers musical worlds of Ceilli, trip hop, tea gardens, and the Mersey beat.[9] Eventually, she finds her father and learns to accept love. Once again, the challenge of this project has been in cross-cultural notions about how theatre is ideally produced. Should work be developed in resident theatres? On university campuses? The UK has a strong system of "research and development," but how does that complement our US context of private funding? In the United States, musical theatre composers usually write lyrics; that is not the norm in the UK. And artistically, how do you tell two sides of a transnational story in a way that works for both sets of audiences? These are some of the challenges, and I do not yet have answers, but the learning curve has been a wonderful journey.

During December 2015 and January 2016 my two collaborators, novelist Richard Aellen and composer Errollyn Wallen, came to the University of Michigan to work with students on developing and recording songs for the show. Two weeks later we traveled to New York City to work with professional actors on a staged reading of the script. Performers in both locations became more culturally aware as they discovered how African cultures, in diaspora, contributed to both American and British histories. The play is written in multiple dialects: Irish, Afro-Caribbean, Jamaican, Liverpudlian, London British, and New York (Brooklyn). As the actors struggled to understand the context for the dialects, they participated in dramaturgical discussions about transatlantic travel, the Windrush generation,[10] and British anti-slavery activism. The creative team talked about black and Irish relationships focusing on how neighboring, multilingual communities supported cultural encounters and racial mixing. Our artistic process of having discussions about the script revealed the diverse cultural heritages of each of the artists in the room. Often, we talked about the actor's migration stories and discussed relatives who could have been affected by these cross-cultural exchanges. Learning about black and Irish experiences in London, New York, Liverpool, and Jamaica reminded all of us about how minimal our degrees of separation across continents are.

Classroom Learning

Working at global sites is challenging and transformative, but we cannot always travel. We spend most of our time working with students in classrooms. How do we bring the global to our daily university lives? The minor I coordinate in Global Theatre and Ethnic Studies depends on finding the global in the local. We travel the world by reading, discussing, and staging plays from the canons of diverse cultural drama. Earlier I discussed the "perform your identity" exercise. This exercise encourages me to value the tremendous amount of diversity that exists among students in my local environment. America is already diverse, but most of us walk in set patterns of encounter that prevent us from interacting with the cultural experiences of the people that surround us. Studio courses in the Global Theatre minor incorporate local visitors as core partners for classroom activities that come to share their expertise. These partners include campus constituencies, community organizations, and student organizations. Campus constituencies are departments and administrative units outside of the theatre department. I lean upon colleagues housed in Latino studies or Asian languages, in religious studies or social work. Campus constituencies can aid in bringing global projects to the mainstage. And this includes possibilities for working across class as well as cultural boundaries. A partnership with campus constituencies might include staging a production with university maintenance workers or having students devise a work about area bus drivers. All of these possibilities will broaden the cultural perspectives of students, faculty members, staff, and administrators. It is about broadening the perspectives of all involved, reconsidering production and performance processes, and expanding the borders of theatrical practices.

Community organizations are often knowledgeable about event planning, and universities can collaborate with them to make plays by figuring out how to exchange expertise. For example, maybe the local church would like to include a song or dance performance in a fundraising event. Even better, perhaps a locally organized music event includes spoken word artists or krumpers[11] who could introduce a new performance style to students. In January 2015, I directed a Puerto Rican play where all of the characters needed to perform parkour. This athletic performance style involves acrobatic leaps, slides, and jumps over physical obstacles. When I began rehearsals I had no idea where I would find someone to teach the art form. To my surprise, the university had a parkour club that I never knew existed. Each time I look for an ethnic art form—in Wisconsin, Tallahassee, upstate New York, or Michigan—I find practitioners hidden in plain sight. Not hidden—merely outside of my own set patterns of encounter. Student organizations hold a wealth of expertise in multicultural performance forms. Although we are the teachers and they are the students, collaborative exchange means respecting their knowledge of folk- and street-based performance and valuing that as theatrical practice. We all know our students are faster with technology than we are. They may also be more culturally astute than we are.

Finding the Global in the Local means expanding our ideas about what theatre is. For some cultures, the storytelling of theatre is captured in outdoor pageants, street competitions, or daylong parades. These genres do not fit neatly inside of the proscenium box, yet they prevail throughout the world. Perhaps it is possible for theatre departments to embrace multiple theatrical styles and use these unfamiliar forms to train students in global theatre. There are exciting developments in training that indicate a shift in pedagogy. Devising is now a part of many department programs. This approach to performance de-privileges the written text, substituting movement, images, and intertextual symbols. With the success of *Hamilton*, more departments are embracing styles like hip-hop and spoken word; Asian movement forms have become a part of some training programs. And there is so much more to explore, such as masking, puppetry, and song as text.

Of course, at the bottom of it all is story. Stories grounded in multicultural performance aesthetics give students a chance to experiment with style and master rigorous techniques for interpreting drama. Stories and the characters they feature matter if we are to really promote diversity of culture and cross-cultural dialogue. For example, the 50/50 by 2020 initiative of the League of Professional Theatre Women aims to achieve parity for professional women theatre artists by the year 2020. The organization recognizes that authorship may impact story and consequently hopes to have regional theatres develop seasons in which at least half of the plays are written by women.[12] The same applies to multicultural theatre. My own theatre department primarily offers minority theatre students opportunities to perform in Eurocentric plays. How do we change that? How do we promote theatre productions by and about people of color as a valuable pursuit for all theatre students—not just students of color?

I advocate bringing multicultural drama to the main stage—not to the studio, not to the outdoor forum, not to the neighboring community. Why? It validates multicultural drama as a core value and an inherently robust site of theatrical tradition. We must work harder to locate under-produced plays. Ethnic communities and their canons cover a broad range of historical styles. It is possible to study melodrama by teaching and staging the 1847 play *The Black Doctor* by Ira Aldridge or to investigate commedia by teaching the *actos* of Luis Valdez. This is not a radical idea. Theatre audiences and their tastes shift with social movements. While realism may have been radical in 1910, it is now all too familiar.

Once again, we can adjust core beliefs about how theatre is made. One way is to offer students opportunities to improvise, devise, and write new theatrical works, perhaps in collaboration with diverse cultural communities. In November 2015, I attended an event about theatre training at the National Theater Institute located at the O'Neill Center in New London, Connecticut. Thirty educators met to discuss how theatre training can prepare students for millennial performance. We shared processes, saw new work, and exchanged ideas. I was most impressed with the industry casting agent who told us that we are *not* effectively training our students for the types of theatre that new playwrights are writing—playwrights like Hansol Jung, Tarell Alvin McCraney, Sharon Bridgforth, Suzan-Lori Parks, Mary Kathryn Nagle, Lin-Manuel Miranda, and Ping Chong. Works by these playwrights require fluidity of expression, physical awareness, an ability to move through theatrical styles like performance art, and an understanding of how to perform a variety of different cultural forms.

We can read these new plays in the classroom and stage them with our students, working beyond our preconceived ideas about how to cast along racial or ethnic lines. All students, by embodying characters outside of their experiences, expand their repertory of available roles. They learn about world cultures through the process of physically enacting the beliefs and behaviors of another person. Ideally, universities are a place where students and faculty members collectively explore new ideas and paradigms for theatrical work as we train students for the theatre's future. Minority theatre did not suddenly appear on the stage as a result of the cultural revolutions of the 1990s. Latino, African American, and Asian artists have been writing, producing, and staging theatrical work for centuries. These canons of literature enrich our understanding of world theatre in a global context.

Finally, how does writing and scholarship fit into the picture? The field is changing. Increasingly I see scholarship that bridges disciplinary boundaries. Many of the authors in this volume have written essays that bring together cultural studies and theatre studies. Scholars are finding linkages between classics, religious studies, and other fields as they consider dramaturgies of diverse world communities. My own scholarship is also informed by collaboration and exchange. This happens in several ways: I engage in dialogic performance when I work with artists, I collaborate

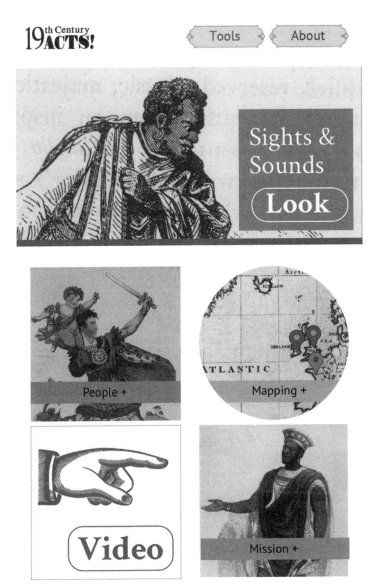

Figure 4. The home page of the interactive website 19thcenturyacts.com. The suite of digital humanities tools allows users to visualize context for nineteenth-century performance and to learn more about underrepresented performers. Home page designed by Clara McClenon.

with archivists at international archives, and I collaborate with teams of librarians and computer scientists on digital tools. By dialogic performance I mean the kinds of exchanges that happen when people encounter one another and share practice to comment about identity. For example, my book *Afro-Mexico: Dancing between Myth and Reality*,[13] examines how indigenous and mestizo populations in Mexico perform African identities, how they dialogue with contemporary Afro-Mexican communities. While researching the book, I traveled to Mexican communities to dance with people. Through the dancing we were able to talk about how the body communicates and what a foot stamp with a head throw might mean for each of us. This embodied research—physical dialogue and exchange—helps me to craft the writing.

My current research is about maritime performance. For this project I have visited maritime archives in New York, London, Bristol, and Liverpool. Even as I mine the archive for information about how sailors performed, I engage with contemporary maritime communities, singing sea shanties at Mystic Seaport and working as a destination lecturer on Caribbean cruise ships.[14] These experiences allow me to write scholarship that considers how different those worlds might be from my daily life while uncovering new information about port and maritime communities. My most complex research project is actually a digital tool, www.19thcenturyacts.com, that I have been developing for about four years now. This tool visually depicts nineteenth-century performance in multiple ways. The mapping tool allows users to see how artists working in the nineteenth century toured in order to make a living. Here, the user can access information about Ira Aldridge, Jenny Lind, or Edwin Booth. The context tool provides images of places and artifacts and gestures to provide a sense of what performances looked and sounded like. I am particularly excited about this section of the tool because it replicates the sense of browsing in the archive in a digital way. The tool demonstrates how even during the nineteenth century, the scope of the English-language performance world was international.

So where have we traveled in this discussion? I talked about collaboration. I talked about research and dialogic partnerships. I talked about communication and embodiment. Most of all, I talked about changing our set patterns of encounter and moving out of our comfort zones, letting go of preconceived notions about what the journey of theatre looks like. We are not all the same. We walk with different religions, class backgrounds, racial experiences, and gender expectations. But we can find common ground within theatrical expressions. To accomplish this, we will need to sit with the unfamiliar, ask disturbing questions, and invest in learning new stories to define our practice. At its core, theatre brings individuals together to explore how life experiences merge into human stories. The journey is most illuminating when we bring a wide spectrum of voices into the "empty space" and recognize that cultural spaces we might imagine as a void are full of a diversity of lived human experiences.[15]

Notes

This paper is adapted from a keynote presentation offered at the SETC Theatre Symposium at Agnes Scott College on April 22, 2016.

1. Gust A. Yep, "Encounters With the 'Other,'" *The Global Intercultural Communication Reader* (New York: Routledge, 2014), 339–56. The entire volume is useful for those embarking on an exchange experience. Also see Lila Abu-Lughod, "Do Muslim Women Really Need Saving? Anthropological Reflections on Cultural Relativism and Its Others," *American Anthropologist* 104, no. 3 (September 2002): 783–90.

2. A video about the meaning and impact of this project is available at: http://ns.umich.edu/new/multimedia/videos/23367-u-m-course-challenges-students-to-learn-about-native-american-culture-through-immersion.

3. Sugar Island is a small island located just east of Sault Ste. Marie on the St. Mary's River. The island is named for the many sugar maple trees that grow there. The Sault Ste. Marie Chippewa Tribe maintains their culture camp and powwow grounds on the island.

4. http://sliverofafullmoon.org/ provides information about the origin of this dramatic work and documents productions at the Smithsonian National Museum of the American Indian, Stanford Law School, New York University, and other locations.

5. In the United Kingdom, citizens of African and Indian ancestry refer to themselves as black communities because the nomenclature around blackness conflates multiple nationalities, ethnicities, and experiences into a single label. The designation of "black" includes British-born blacks, South Asians from India and Pakistan, Africans coming from countries such as Somalia, Nigeria, Ghana, and Sudan, as well as Jamaicans and Afro-Caribbean descendants.

6. Information about these vibrant cultural organizations can be found at the following websites: http://www.africaoye.com, http://www.brouhaha.uk.com, https://www.facebook.com/The-Greenhouse-Multi-Cultural-Play-and-Arts-Project-194745240596801, http://www.granbysomaliwomensgroup.org, http://www.theblack-e.co.uk, and http://www.mdi.org.uk/

7. The performance video of the show, called "Framing Liverpool through Michigan Eyes," can be viewed at https://www.youtube.com/watch?v=qOxHbbkXUac.

8. http://www.liverpooltrading.com

9. Ceilli is a form of Irish folk music. Trip hop is a music style that originated in Bristol that blends electronic music with soul, funk, jazz, and Jamaican ska. The African Grove theatre, known as the first African American theatre company,

was founded in 1821 in a tea garden in New York City. Finally, Mersey Beat is the musical sound associated with the Beatles that began during the late 1950s when service workers on transatlantic passenger ships brought African American music records to dance clubs in Liverpool.

10. The Empire Windrush was a ship that brought Jamaican settlers to England between 1948 and 1954 to rebuild the country's infrastructure after World War II. Jamaican immigrants who arrived during this historical time are known as the "Windrush" generation.

11. Krumping is an urban dance style with percussive upper body moves performed with improvisation.

12. http://theatrewomen.org/programs/5050-in-2020-parity-for-women-theatre-artists.

13. Anita Gonzalez, *Afro-Mexico: Dancing Between Myth and Reality* (Austin, University of Texas Press, 2010).

14. Mystic Seaport is a maritime museum located in Mystic, Connecticut, where visitors and scholars work and study with actual vessels. My work as a destination cruise lecturer involves traveling to Caribbean ports and educating passengers about the history and cultures of the ports.

15. Here I reference Peter Brook's foundational book *The Empty Space* (New York: Touchstone Press, 1992). His book proposes that the theatre is an empty space to be filled by the actor and director's imagination. Here, I suggest that Peter Brook's "empty space" could be opened to include cultures and communities outside of his imagined Eurocentric experiences.

Certain Kinds of Dances

Used among Them

An Initial Inquiry into Colonial
Spanish Encounters with the *Areytos*
of the *Taíno* in Puerto Rico

E. Bert Wallace

"The earliest known performance of a European play in the Americas took place at a seminary in Puerto Rico in 1510."[1] Before happening upon the above passage while looking for something else, now forgotten, I did not know much about the island of Puerto Rico other than that it had some sort of American territorial status, that Puerto Ricans are American citizens who cannot vote, and that Rita Moreno and Tito Puente came from there. The passage struck me as odd: the date seemed off and I could not find it confirmed anywhere. My curiosity was piqued; this ultimately led to several trips to the island for archival research and conference presentations. Eventually, I found conclusively that the statement could not be true (it is just too early for any such activity in Puerto Rico),[2] but my interest in Puerto Rico generally and Spanish colonial theatre practice there more specifically had been sparked.

There is precious little archival information on the island of Puerto Rico itself: most of the surviving records are housed in the *Archivo General de Indias* in Seville, Spain. That research is ongoing, but the focus of this paper is yet another offshoot of my initial line of inquiry. Research revealed hints by chroniclers from the colonial period and contemporary Puerto Rican scholars that the Spanish friars made attempts to Christianize the *areyto*, a traditional *Taíno* performance, in their evangelistic efforts. My research interests in religion and theatre, in addition to a desire to understand more about the aboriginal inhabitants of Puerto Rico, led me to investigate further.

A very brief history of the colonization of Puerto Rico is in order here. My focus is particularly on Puerto Rico, though of course the rest of the Greater Antilles and the continents of North and South America figure much more prominently in the larger colonization story. Puerto Rico was sighted by Christopher Columbus on his second, much-better-funded voyage to the New World in 1493. There were seventeen ships and approximately 1,500 men, including the chronicler Fray Ramón Pane, whose *Relación de Fray Ramón* is our earliest firsthand account of Puerto Rico. The *Relación* has value, but later accounts question its validity (along with much of Pane's works): he wrote it in Castilian (not his native dialect) and the original is lost anyway. A more comprehensive contemporary chronicle is Fray Bartolomé de las Casa's *Brevisima relación de las destruccíon de las Indias.* Though Bartolomé spent all of his time in the New World on Hispaniola (now the Dominican Republic and Haiti), his father Pedro was with Columbus on the second voyage. Later chronicles by Gonzalo Fernandez de Oviedo y Valdes and Pedro Mártir de Angelería ("Peter Martyr") are also valuable.[3]

After sailing through the Lesser Antilles, Columbus sighted Puerto Rico on November 19, though no written record shows us that he actually set foot on the island. He certainly saw it—Puerto Rico is the first landmass of any size you hit when sailing in this direction from Spain. Early explorers found the island plentifully inhabited with people they called *Taíno*, based on a word the inhabitants used when greeting the white men. Various sources translate the word as "good" or "brave people" or "peace" (used as a salutation).[4] The *Taínos* called themselves and the island *Borinquen.*[5] Contemporaneous estimates of the *Taíno* population ranged from 30,000 to an improbable eight million; 500,000 to one million is likely a good guess.[6] Columbus named the island San Juan Bautista, and the port city that was established was called Puerto Rico (literally, rich or bounteous port). The names switched later largely due to marketing efforts by Ponce de Leon, the island's second governor.

Among observations made by European explorers of the cultural practices of the *Taíno* were accounts of the Spanish-named *areyto* (or *arieto*). These were described by Oviedo y Valdez as "a good and noble manner of remembering things past and ancient...with the songs and dances."[7] Bartolomé describes the *areyto* similarly, focusing on song, dance, and remembrance: "And on this island what I could understand was that their songs, which they call 'areytos,' were their history passed from person to person, fathers to sons from the present to the future, as here uniting many Indians...passing three or four hours or more until the teacher or guide of the dance finished the history, and sometimes they went from one day to the next."[8] Fray Pane gives us more of a sense of the theatrical nature of the *areyto*. He reports that they included enactments of the *Taíno* creation story as well as ceremonial offerings to the various *cemi* (spirit-idols) of the *Taíno*, including offerings to appease the sky dwellers in the season of *Huracán*.[9]

Cuban scholar Fernando Ortiz describes the *areytos* as consisting of "music, dance, and pantomime applied to religious liturgy, magical rites, epic narratives, tribal histories and expressions of collective will."[10] In the end, the precise nature of what was being described in these accounts is unclear. As Thompson suggests: "First, we have the *areyto* described as ritual, [then] as celebration, as narration, as work song, as a vehicle for teaching a value system, as funeral observance, as social dance, as history lesson, as fertility rite, or simply as a drunken party."[11] He further suggests that the word might have indicated merely "group" or "activity."[12] To date, we do not know exactly what was included. The *areytos* of the *Taínos*, and the *Taínos* themselves, in fact died out. Performances of the *areyto* in Puerto Rico have been revived with some gusto in the *Taíno/Borinquen* identity movement, but the modern pageants must finally be considered speculative. However, all surviving descriptions lead to the not unreasonable conclusion that at least para-theatrical enactment (if not fully theatrical representation) was a significant aspect of the *areyto*. This conclusion can be reached in part due to use of terminology (by Bartolomé and other chroniclers) indicating equivalence between the *areytos* and European theatre and dance: "Castilian-language writers [describing *areytos*] used terms from their own tradition such as *bailes*, *entremeses*, *teatro*, *representates* ['dances,' 'theatrical performances,' 'theatre,' 'actors'] as if they were transparent and universally valid."[13] Because "all terminology represents a history of practice,"[14] it is clear that those original European observers recognized theatrical practice in the *areytos*.

The second element of this study requires a return to my woefully (but necessarily) brief history. Columbus died back in Spain in 1506. Two years later, the first governor of Puerto Rico was in place, and Ferdinand II sent Ponce de Leon to explore the island. After some trouble with Columbus's son Diego (who tried and initially failed to get a grant giving him control over all the land claimed by his father), Ponce was made governor in 1509. That same year, the *repartimiento* system began, allotting specified numbers of *Taíno* to leaders and colonists for so many hours of unpaid labor per day and per season. Local priests sent reports of terrible abuses back to Spain, resulting in the establishment by the Spanish Crown of a new system, *encomienda*. This system, which literally translates "entrustment," is a sort of covenant between stronger and weaker parties enumerating rights and responsibilities of both conquered and conqueror. *Ecomienda* required both that the colonists pay wages to the Indians and that they teach them the Christian religion. The end result of all this was still further abuses and abject slavery, leading to bloody uprisings by the *Taíno* in 1511, in which thousands were executed under Ponce's orders. In 1512, continued attempts to ease the sufferings of the *Taíno* came through Spanish legislation, though these laws were not followed in spirit. However, in an interesting development, in 1514 permission was granted for Spaniards to marry *Taíno* women. Though intermarriage was not common in New World colonies, permission granted implies permission sought. This is consistent with Puerto Rico's history (which continues to this day) of regular racial mingling.

In something of an aside, it is interesting to note that the long-held understanding that the *Taíno* were exterminated by oppression, slavery, and a belief that the *Taíno* were at best sub-human (a belief that facilitated abuses such as amputation of the hands and feet of rabble-rousers) has been belied by a 2000 study by Dr. Juan Martinez Cruzado, funded by the US National Science Foundation. This study demonstrated that 61 percent of all Puerto Ricans today have Amerindian mitochondrial DNA.[15] Though the loss of the *Taíno* culture is significant and should not be minimized, the 1514 sanction of intermarriage ultimately resulted in the absorption of the *Taíno* into the colonial population rather than their outright extinction.

As mentioned, in addition to embryonic attempts at social justice, the *encomienda* required the teaching of the Christian religion to the pagan *Taíno*. This emphasis, for good or ill, was present from the earliest encounters between the colonists and the *Taíno* and was connected to the *areyto* from very early days. Fray Bartolomé, in an extended passage written in the voice of the *Taíno cacique* (chief) Hathuey, records the following event on the island of Cuba: "[Hathuey addresses his followers:] You are not ignorant that there is a rumor spread abroad among us of the Spaniards [*sic*] arrival, and are sensible by woeful experience how such and such [he names them] and *Hayti* [Hispaniola/Haiti] with their Inhabitants have been treated by them, that they design to visit us with equal intentions of committing such acts as they have hitherto been guilty of. But do you not know the cause and reason of their coming?"[16] Hathuey's listeners reply that "we are altogether ignorant of it...but sufficiently satisfied that they are cruelly and wickedly inclined."[17] Hathuey continues: "They adore a certain Covetous Deity, whose cravings are not to be satisfied by a few moderate offerings. That they may answer his Adoration and Worship, [they] demand many unreasonable things of us, and use their utmost endeavors to subjugate and afterwards murder us. [He lifts up a cabinet full of gold and jewels.] This is the Spaniards [*sic*] God, and in honor of him if you think well of it, let us celebrate our *Areytos*...[and] by this means his Deity being appeas'd, he will impose his Commands on the Spaniards that they shall not for the future molest us."[18] Bartolomé describes the *areytos* here as "certain kinds of Dances and caprings [*sic*] used among them."[19] Continuing with his account, Bartolomé writes that all present "unanimously with one consent in a loud tone made this reply: Well said, Well said" and "continued skipping and dancing before this Cabinet, without the least intermission, till they were quite tired and grown weary."[20] Bartolomé's description represents the earliest known connection between an *areyto* and the faith of the colonists. While it was held in response to both the evangelistic message and imperialistic behavior of the Spaniards, no Christian witnessed this particular *areyto* (at least, no European Christian—the presence of any converted *Taíno* is unknown). Indeed, Hathuey concluded that the *Taínos* would probably be destroyed by the Spaniards no matter what, and so decided ("upon mature deliberation") to throw the treasure chest into the river.[21]

It is from a later chronicler, Antonio de Herrera, copying liberally from Bartolomé, who in turn credited Pedro Mártir (Peter Martyr), that we get the first account of direct Christian interaction with an *areyto*: "A sailor is left behind with a group of friendly *Taínos* because of illness as his companions go on a journey. He teaches the *Taínos* some of the basic elements of Christian worship, especially the veneration of the Virgin Mary. He draws an image of the Virgin, reciting, 'Ave Maria, Ave Maria.' The Indians are persuaded to construct a church with an altar dedicated to the Virgin, before which offerings of food and water are placed, in case she should become hungry. The chief and his people enter, kneel, and show great devotion to the Virgin, in whose honors they then compose songs and dances, repeating the words, 'Ave Maria.'"[22] While there is no evidence that this particular performance was directly connected to any subsequent efforts to employ the *areyto* form for Christian purposes, the chronicler specifically used the term "*areyto*" in describing the event.

It is tempting to speculate about the how the *areytos* influenced and interacted with the European performative activities of the colonists such as saint's day processionals, bullfights, and social dances. This is also the period of the great *autos sacramentales* (religious dramas) in Golden Age Spain. We know that *autos* were performed in the New World, though they were eventually banned due to the revelry and drunkenness (inclusive of some priests) that often accompanied them. Given that evangelism was a goal of the *conquistadores*, and was indeed mandated by Spain, it seems possible (even likely) that the Christian friars adapted native traditions in attempts to convert the *Taíno*. While the treatment of the *Taíno*

was appalling, many of the friars were vocally opposed to it: Fray Bartolomé has been described as one of the most hated men in early colonial America because of his opposition to and defiant and very public re-
porting of the atrocities.[23] The churchmen themselves seem to have had
a genuine concern for the souls of the natives, and, unlike the Puritans,
were certainly not hostile to drama.

In this early period, what was happening theatrically in Puerto Rico is
very murky indeed. What is clear is that early colonists were aware of and
influenced by the *areytos*. It is not unlikely that the similarity of the *areytos*
to the pageantry of the *autos* and the mystery plays performed throughout
Europe would have been recognized. It was also not unusual for colonial
authorities to "Christianize" various aspects of aboriginal culture. Fray
Bartolomé, who was well aware of both Christian evangelistic efforts and
the religious practices of the *Taíno*, personally observed *areyto* performances and understood their significance for a doomed people: "There
is no greater token among [the *Taíno*] than this of their extraordinary ex-
ultation and rejoicing...nor will they, 'til the General Conflagration, ever
discontinue the celebration of these festivals and the lamentations and
singing with certain kinds of rhythms in their *areytos*, the doleful ditties
of calamity and ruin."[24] As evidenced here, a cultural practice pursued so
doggedly by the *Taíno* would not have escaped the notice of the Church.

The colonists were interested in evangelization of and intermarriage
with the *Taíno* and were certainly aware of the *areytos*. Though it is yet
to be determined exactly what the intercultural relationship between the
religious and theatrical consisted of, available evidence makes such an exchange seem inevitable. Though the history of European interaction with
the aboriginal peoples of the New World is often ignoble, with many colonists considering them sub-human, these observations by Spanish chroniclers recognize the *areytos* as legitimate (if primitive, by their standards)
artistic expression. This recognition, and the probable adoption of at least
some aspect of the *areyto* by the Catholic Church, suggests an at least la-
tent recognition of the humanity of the people they had come to conquer.

My own work on the intersection of religion and theatre, which has
been largely grounded in Western traditions, has been expanded by this
research, particularly toward how the *autos* were performed in both the
Old and New Worlds and how those two spheres influenced each other.
A chance reading of an erroneous sentence has resulted in knowledge
and understanding of a culture of which I was almost completely un-
ware. Though success is never guaranteed, and frustration inevitable, the
scholar should be willing to follow rabbit trails. They can lead to remarkable places where the natives of strange new worlds dance and caper.

Notes

1. Oscar G. Brockett and Franklin Hildy, *History of the Theatre* (Boston: Allyn and Bacon, 2008), 150.

2. I contacted Franklin Hildy about the error; he has acknowledged that the statement is not correct.

3. Donald Thompson, "The 'Cronistas de Indias' Revisited: Historical Reports, Archeological Evidence, and Literary and Artistic Traces of Indigenous Music and Dance in the Greater Antilles at the Time of the 'Conquista,'" *Latin American Music Review* 14, no. 2 (Autumn-Winter 1993): 181–201. Though a musicological study, Thompson's work is very valuable in understanding the *Taíno areytos*.

4. For more information on the *Taíno* language, see the online *Modern Taíno Dictionary* (http://www.taino-tribe.org/tedict.html) and the website of the *Jatibonicu Taíno* Tribal Nation of Borikén (http://www.taino-tribe.org/jatibonicu-flagstory.htm).

5. It should be noted that the *Taíno* people that I discuss here did not reside solely on Puerto Rico (sociologists refer to the Puerto Rican and Hispaniola *Taíno* as "Classic *Taíno*," those in modern Jamaica, Cuba, and the Bahamas as "Western *Taíno*," and those in the Northern Lesser Antilles as "Eastern *Taíno*," not to mention those in Florida and elsewhere).

6. See Noble David Cook, *Born to Die: Disease and New World Conquest 1493–1650* (Cambridge: Cambridge University Press, 1998).

7. Quoted in Galen Brokaw, "Ambivalence, Mimicry, and Stereotype in Fernández de Oviedo's *Historia general y natural de las Indias: Colonial Discourse and the Caribbean Areito,*" *CR: The New Centennial Review* 5, no. 3 (2005): 143–65.

8. Bartolomé de las Casas, *Brevisima relación de las destruccion de las Indias* (Seville, 1552; English trans., London: R. Hewson, 1689), Project Gutenberg, 2007, https://www.gutenberg.org/ebooks/20321.

9. For good summaries of *Taíno* and other Caribbean religious beliefs and practices, see Diana Taylor, "Scenes of Cognition: Performance and Conquest," *Theatre Journal* 56, no. 3 (October 2004): 353–72, and Hartley Burr Alexander, ed., "Latin American Mythology," in *Mythology of All Races*, ed. Herbert Louis Grey, vol. 11 (Boston: Marshall Jones Company, 1920).

10. Author's translation of "*come conjunto de musica, baile y pantomime aplicado a las liturgias religiosas, a los ritos magicos, a las narraciones epopeyicas, a las historias tribalaes y las grandes expressions be la voluntad colectiva.*" Quoted from Fernando Ortiz, "Preluldios ethico de la música afrocubana," *Los instrumentos de la música afrocubana*, 5 vols. (La Habana: Ministerio de Educación, Dirección de Cultura, 1952–1955).

11. Thompson, "The 'Cronistas de Indias' Revisited," 187–88.

12. Ibid.

13. Taylor, "Scenes of Cognition," 355–56.

14. Ibid.

15. "Recent Research Contributions of Genetics to the Studies of Population

History and Anthropology in Puerto Rico," *Profiles* 1, no. 2 (August 15, 2000), http://www.taino-tribe.org/pr-taino-dna.htm.

16. De las Casas, *Brevisima relación de las destruccíon de las Indias.*

17. Ibid.

18. Ibid.

19. Ibid.

20. Ibid.

21. Ibid.

22. Quoted in Thompson, "The 'Cronistas de Indias' Revisited," 192.

23. This is an often-used descriptor of Fray Bartolomé. For an excellent article on this subject, see Hartono Budi, "Bartolome de las Casas and the Question of Evangelization," *Jurnal Teologi* 2, no. 1 (May 2013): 49–57.

24. De las Casas, *Brevisima relación de las destruccíon de las Indias.*

Gertrude Hoffmann's Lawful Piracy

"A Vision of Salome" and the Russian Season as Transatlantic Production Impersonations

Sunny Stalter-Pace

Dance is a form of performance in which we regularly see what Zora Neale Hurston calls "the exchange and re-exchange of ideas between groups."[1] There is a lot of excellent scholarship tracing the genealogies of cross-cultural dialogue within different dance forms, from Brian Seibert's massive tome on tap dancing to Priya Srinivasan's discussion of Indian *nachwalis* or nautch dancers in *Sweating Saris*.[2] These books consider how dance circulates across classes and nations, as well as how its meaning changes depending on who is doing the performing. In her recent book *Choreographing Copyright*, Anthea Kraut refocuses critical attention on the moments when creators attempt to shut down this exchange and reexchange through legal action. They do so, she argues, in response to "a perceived crisis: not the crisis posed by dance's disappearance (as an influential strand of dance and performance studies theory posits) but the peril of its reproduction."[3] Rather than emphasizing dance's ephemerality, a focus on copyright emphasizes, and tries to control, its reproducibility.

This article focuses on a performer and producer who made a career out of such perilous reproductions. Gertrude Hoffmann (1885–1966) was an American dancer, comedienne, choreographer, and producer.[4] Above all, though, she was a mimic. Hoffmann's first vaudeville turns imitated the characteristic songs and patter of other stage celebrities of the time, both male and female.[5] Later, lavish revues by Hoffmann included imitations of Ruth St. Denis and Isadora Duncan dances. After German theatrical innovator Max Reinhardt visited the United States to perform *Sumurun* in 1912, Hoffmann put on a streamlined version of his Orientalist pantomime in a Brooklyn vaudeville house. In the later part of her career, Hoffmann managed a dance troupe called the Gertrude Hoffmann Girls.

They played the Moulin Rouge in Paris, filled out Broadway revues, and performed nightclub routines into the 1940s in New York City and Chicago. Their most-celebrated dance routines used props and techniques from circus acrobatics and sabre fencing.[6] Hoffmann's career brings to light the complications of copying.

Hoffmann made her name in America by performing unauthorized copies of dances she had seen in Europe. The performance that brought her national fame in 1908 was a copied Dance of the Seven Veils called "A Vision of Salome." Maud Allan was then giving her Salome dance at the Palace Theatre in London; Hoffmann's act was billed as "an exact imitation" and "a life-like impersonation" of it.[7] She followed this with an even more audacious imitation, a fully realized copy of Michel Fokine's dances for Serge Diaghilev's Ballets Russes that debuted in New York City in 1911 and toured the country through early 1912. Hoffmann's ersatz Russian ballet toured the United States five years before Diaghilev's troupe arrived. (Early advertisements called the production "Saison Des Ballets Russes," but henceforth I call it the Russian Season for clarity's sake.) Hoffmann may not have been an innovator according to contemporary standards, but she was a tastemaker, and she brought the first performances of the dance as a total work of art to the American stage. Why does she not play a bigger role in the histories of American dance and performance?

Hoffmann has been assigned a minor part, I argue, because of her questionable borrowing practices. Her performances blurred the line between cross-cultural exchange and copyright violation, engaging in what copyright scholar Robert Spoo dubs "lawful piracy."[8] He uses the term to cover reproduction of material that falls within the public domain in one country though it is subject to copyright law in others. Hoffmann's performances of "A Vision of Salome" and the Russian Season were brazen, but they were not illegal; as such, they help us understand the slipperiness of the public domain in early twentieth-century American performance. Only by examining performance that falls into legal and moral grey areas can we fully understand the historically and culturally specific processes of appropriation and dissemination. "Exchange and reexchange" does not always take place with the consent of both parties.

"A Vision of Salome" and the Russian Season show us that unethical artistic exchange can nevertheless have a major impact. Although the former was a solo number and the latter a three-hour production with hundreds of cast and crew members, these two dances should be understood in dialogue with one another. In both cases, Hoffmann traveled to Europe, observed an influential dance performance there, replicated both the choreography and production design, and toured the United States with her imitation. With these dances Hoffmann engages in two strategies of "lawful piracy" that are worthy of note: production impersonation and transatlantic imitation.

I take the term "production impersonation" from an early review of Hoffmann's vaudeville routine. Her imitation of Adeline Genée's hunting dance initially included a cinematic projection and seven men on horseback. Keep in mind this was for one bit in a twenty-minute act. The "Hunting Dance," a *Variety* review suggests, "entitles Miss Hoffmann to the distinction of being the only 'production impersonator.'"[9] This was a production that went beyond being a showcase for one performer's mimetic faculties. Instead, it became a testament to Hoffmann's ability to see a performance and replicate an important number in its totality. Like a shot-for-shot remake, it humbled itself before an original and showily proclaimed its own skill at the same time. Production impersonation differs from mimicry that happens on the bodily level, such as one performer imitating another's steps. Instead, production impersonation copies the setting, costumes, and staging as well as physical movement; it attempts to recreate the full sensual experience of watching the original production.

The meaning and impact of Hoffmann's production impersonations shifted when she began to imitate European performances rather than American ones. Hoffmann's earliest imitations, even those with a heavy production element, were acts of physical virtuosity understood within a shared framework of performance conventions local to American vaudeville. In order to observe the earliest subjects of her imitations, Gertrude Hoffmann merely had to travel across town: George M. Cohan, Eva Tanguay, and *The Merry Widow*, whose waltz she copied, all played in local theatres. But her "Dance of the Seven Veils" marks a shift to transatlantic appropriation, one that continued with the Russian Season. Instead of commenting on an original that could just as easily be seen across town, Hoffmann's later work established the context for the original while it was still across the Atlantic.

Transatlantic imitation took advantage of the increased mobility between the United States and Europe at the dawn of the twentieth century. In *Transatlantic Broadway*, Marlis Schweitzer discusses the ways that ocean liners "encouraged the globalization of theatrical practices and cultures."[10] The ocean liner had secured an amplified importance in this period, since increasing speed made it easier to move back and forth between the great theatrical cities. This was a period when Europe was "scoured for acts" that would bring class and authenticity to the American vaudeville stage.[11] Performers and producers who were able to circulate between the two continents leveraged their early access to performances abroad, using "what economists call first-mover advantage."[12] This means they used their early access to European performances in order to create imitation American performances, imitations that could then circulate through America before the original arrived.[13]

Gertrude Hoffmann made at least three Atlantic crossings between 1908 and 1911, one to observe Maud Allan's performance and two to observe the Ballets Russes and solicit participation from former Imperial Russian dancers. After seeing the Diaghilev production, Hoffmann felt inspired to bring these dances to the United States, "resolv[ing]" that it was her "special task to introduce this new and most brilliant form of terpsichorean art to the American people."[14] She did make that initial introduction, though it was not through the usual channels of cross-cultural exchange. Theatrical managers and talent scouts might offer lavish contracts to European music hall stars (like Scottish comedian Harry Lauder) or purchase the American rights to a European play (like *The Merry Widow*). But Hoffmann did not pay for Maud Allan or Diaghilev's company to come to the United States. She did not buy the rights to the choreography (which, after all, was not protected under US law). Instead, she engaged in transatlantic production impersonation.

Thus far, "A Vision of Salome" and the Russian Season have been talked about in very different ways. Since Elizabeth Kendall's *Where She Danced*, critics have acknowledged the originality in Hoffmann's version of the Dance of the Seven Veils. In that book, Kendall says "her Salomé, begun as an imitation, became the first coherent dance creation since Isadora Duncan had left the country in 1900 and Ruth St. Denis in 1906."[15] Hoffmann's imitations in the Russian Season have been judged far more harshly. Kendall credits Hoffmann with bringing the Ballets Russes to the United States in an "elaborate but pirated edition."[16] Hoffmann's 1966 obituary in *Dance Magazine* notes the "dubious professional ethics involved" in her uncredited imitations of Fokine.[17] A more recent book by Sharyn Udall also calls the Russian Season "pirated" and gives credit for the production to "the unscrupulous if enterprising American dancer Gertrude Hoffmann."[18] But the unscrupulous imitation of the Russian Season engages in the same performance practices as "A Vision of Salome," reproducing them on a larger scale, albeit without giving credit to the choreographer.

By engaging in a thick description of the theatrical practices of borrowing that led to Hoffmann's "A Vision of Salome" dance and the imitations of the Russian Season, I hope to counteract the tendency to dismiss art whose practices of citation were not in line with contemporary standards. Of course, I borrow the notion of "thick description" from Clifford Geertz, who borrows it in turn from British philosopher Gilbert

Ryle.[19] It is the anthropologist's job, Geertz says, to establish the cultural frameworks in which the same gesture might be understood differently. In Gertrude Hoffmann's case, it is necessary to thickly describe a few cultural arguments surrounding popular performance in the period in order to understand her copying practices in their own context.

Gertrude Hoffmann's piracy did not happen in a vacuum. It was an extension of the theatrical culture of the period and of her career on the vaudeville stage. Several legal conditions encouraged Hoffmann's copying: the United States did not sign on to the international author's rights protections of the Berne Convention until 1988 and lacked bilateral copyright agreements with Russia.[20] Broader cultural and theatrical trends played their part as well, from the success of Viennese operetta *The Merry Widow* in 1907 to the mania for Russian dances in the wake of Pavlova and Mordkin's American tour of 1910.[21] And of course there was the broader imitative culture of vaudeville itself, where according to Susan Glenn "every conceivable kind of comic imitation was in full flower: blackface minstrelsy, gender impersonation, burlesque, parody, and ethnic caricature."[22] Hoffmann's work highlights a transitional period in American popular performance when residual traditions from the freewheeling and performer-centered nineteenth century clashed with those of the producer-centered twentieth century.[23]

By tracing Hoffmann's transatlantic travels and the production impersonations that arose from them, we see both the cultural parameters of the period and the kinds of work it was possible to produce within them. In the following discussion of "A Vision of Salome," we see how transatlantic production impersonation functions within a solo performance. The subsequent section shows how these techniques translated to the Russian Season. The conclusion suggests some of the reasons that Hoffmann's imitations matter, particularly in an era when unauthorized copies tend to be mediated through digital technologies rather than the bodies of performers who have traveled abroad.

Recently, dance studies scholars have begun to think through "A Vision of Salome" in relation to a broader trend of cultural appropriation, which Marlis Schweitzer calls the "Salome epidemic."[24] In the early twentieth century, the American popular stage was overrun with "Dance of the Seven Veils" knockoffs performed by all manner of Salomes. These dances had their roots in late nineteenth-century performance, combining the lowbrow exotica of Little Egypt with the highbrow bombast of Wagner and Wilde, in differing proportions. Fanny Brice and Eva Tanguay performed comic takes on the dance; Julian Eltinge performed one in drag and blackface. Most of these dances were notable because of the brevity

of the dancers' costumes, though Aida Overton Walker performed a re-
fined version with little nudity to speak of.[25] But Gertrude Hoffmann's
performance stood apart.

In 1908 Maud Allan performed her Salome dance in London to massive acclaim and scandal. Oscar Hammerstein wanted his own version before one of his rivals signed Allan to an American contract. Hoffmann
traveled to London at Hammerstein's behest to observe Maud Allan's
choreography and set design "with a view to future imitation."[26] She observed the production in totality, from its choreography to its set design
to its lighting cues, and replicated it in New York City with her dance "A
Vision of Salome." Hoffmann's take on the "Dance of the Seven Veils"
was seen both as one of the most imitative and one of the most remarkable versions of the dance. Mary Simonson called Gertrude Hoffmann
"the true star of the American Salome dancers," observing that her dance
alone combined seriousness and humor, originality and imitation.[27] This
was "borrowed art," to be sure, but it revealed that Hoffmann was an
original performer and producer.[28]

Critics of the period found Hoffmann's "A Vision of Salome" notable
for its creation of a mood that ran through the choreography, music, and
set design. A review in the July 14, 1908, edition of the *New York World*
called it "a model of stage manager's art" with "wondrous scenic investi-
ture, dreamy, sensuous music composed by her husband and magnificent
stage management."[29] For Hoffmann, imitation did not merely mean replicating the physical and verbal tics of a performer; it meant replicating the
whole mood of their performance through set design, costume design,
and music. In this way, she offered a mimetic alternative to Belascoism,
where instead of reproducing settings for their fidelity to "real life," they
were reproduced for their fidelity to another stage production.[30] We can
understand "A Vision of Salome" as part of a shared stage culture where
the audience was cognizant of the absent original she was imitating. The
staging of this dance is also important because it anticipates her interest
in the Ballets Russes productions as total works of art.

Hoffmann's production impersonation came to fruition in the Russian Season. Unlike Maud Allan's Salome dance, the Ballets Russes performances could not be imitated based on Gertrude Hoffmann's observations alone. The designs were too complex and the costumes had too
much detail; the movement vocabulary of those trained in Imperial Russian ballet techniques was too different from her own. Hoffmann studied
with a Russian ballet master in Paris and brought him back to New York
with her so that she could do a better job of replicating the new forms
of movement in the dances. Costumes were recreated by Marie Muelle,
based on Bakst's designs.[31] Hoffmann and her manager and co-producer

Morris Gest hired away dancers who were involved with the original production, including Lydia Lopokova and Theodore Kosloff.[32] Kosloff served as the choreographer and dance director for Hoffmann's production; he also played several roles in the show, including that of the Golden Slave, which had been played by Nijinsky in Paris. They used the original music from the Paris shows, albeit as arranged by Hoffmann's bandleader husband, Max. And with two years' worth of salary from the vaudeville stage, she, along with impresarios Morris Gest and F. Ray Comstock, paid for a production that included over 200 cast and crew members.[33]

This peculiar production debuted at New York's Winter Garden Theatre in July 1911 and toured the United States into early 1912, reaching Americans from New York to San Francisco. It mimicked the first and second season of Diaghilev's Paris ballets in as much detail as could be managed. The program featured uncredited imitations of three ballets choreographed by Michel Fokine: *Cléopâtre*, *Les Sylphides*, and *Schéhérazade*. But its first advertisement gave over far more space to emphasizing the size of its cast and their transatlantic credentials. It gave a "Partial List of the Most Prominent and Internationally Famous Artists in the Organization": some were former dancers with Diaghilev's troupe, others were members of the *corps* at the Grand Opera House in Paris, and still others had been trained as part of the Imperial theatre systems of Russia and Czechoslovakia.[34] Though the dances may have been new to America, not all the dancers were. Theodore Kosloff had already toured in the United States; according to some sources, the chorus was filled out with American dancers who took on Russian and French pseudonyms.[35] Hoffmann, not a trained ballet dancer, played the mostly pantomimed roles made famous by Ida Rubinstein—Cleopatra and Zobeide (the favorite wife of the sultan in *Schéhérazade*).

The Russian Season made an impact on American theatre not yet reflected in the critical discussion of the work. It was not the first time Russian dances had been presented in America, but it was the first time that Russian ballet had been presented as a fully staged spectacle, one worthy of consideration as a piece of theatre. The impact of this impersonated production was recognized in its day. A magazine article from 1918 included Hoffmann's Russian Season in the genealogy of the modern theatre with such canonical masters of modern drama as William Butler Yeats and Max Reinhardt. Early twentieth-century theatre critic and translator Sam Eliot Jr. described it as follows: "The Russian ballets, presented by Gertrude Hoffmann with the novel, glaring costumes and scenes of Leon Bakst. Color in artistic patterns for its own sake, so to speak, was a new revelation to America. The successful coalescence of dance-drama, music, and color-art taught us much about synthesis and unity on the stage, started a new breed of artists toward stage-designing, and gave even the vaudeville public a new esthetic [*sic*] criterion."[36] Eliot highlighted a number of qualities in the Russian Season that became valued as part of the New Stagecraft: abstraction, aesthetic unity, and non-naturalistic use of color. Although each of the three ballets included within the Russian Season had a different style, that style was reflected across all parts of the performance. Each dance attempted to evoke a mood through all elements of stagecraft, from music to costumes to sets to movement. Hoffmann introduced American vaudeville audiences to modernist performance.

The Russian Season's influence reverberated through early twentieth-century American performing arts, especially through the European design aesthetic it brought to the stage and the Orientalism it brought to the screen. Famed set designer Robert Edmond Jones saw the show when he was still at Harvard and designed costumes for Hoffmann's next revue, *From Broadway to Paris*.[37] Hoffmann's dance director Theodore Kosloff settled in Los Angeles; he collaborated with Cecil B. DeMille in the 1920s, helping to establish the look of American exoticism in Hollywood.[38] The influence of the Russian Season may have been overlooked in part because its impact was on the environment and atmosphere of American performance, rather than content or technique. But it was certainly overlooked because of its status as a work of lawful piracy.

Hoffmann's transatlantic production impersonations interrupt and complicate narratives about modernist performance. "A Vision of Salome" and the Russian Season separate innovation from cultural diffusion, reminding us that the pirates, borrowers, and copycats are the ones who often make the most impact. They help us think about how unauthorized cultural borrowing gives work a broader audience. And in the present day, when piracy is most often thought about as a digital form of copying, Hoffmann's work highlights the embodiment that is always a part of copying, though in her case it played a larger part than most.

Hoffmann's copies traded on the value of the originals while emphasizing her versatility and virtuosity: no other performer could present an exotic "snake dance" and then sing a dialect song in the style of Scottish comic Harry Lauder. In this way, Hoffmann operates in a complex position in relation to her audience: she communicates the glamour of someone who has seen the original version but shares the sense of humor with the rube who is only going to see the copy. As such, she mediates between high and low culture in a way that merits further study.

Hoffmann's transatlantic production impersonations illustrate the many ways that global theatrical culture makes its way into the United States. That first transmission often takes a form other than original performance.

Newspaper stories and drawings, sheet music and recordings, and live acts like Gertrude Hoffmann's played equally important roles in the reproduction of early twentieth-century transatlantic theatrical culture. Because of the prevalence of mass media reproductions of performances, "most American audiences experienced plays and performers long before they saw them 'live' or in person."[39] The "Vision of Salome" and the Russian Season, then, offer us particularly salient examples of performance as mediation, a screen for understanding an otherwise unreachable original. Both strategies play with ideas of presence and absence that are at the heart of performance studies.[40]

In the new ecology of transatlantic performance, no one's act was safe from being copied overseas. Even during a trip taken for the purpose of lawful piracy, Gertrude and Max Hoffmann saw its effects on their own careers. Their trip to Europe in the summer of 1910 received particular attention from the New York City newspapers. A dockside interview published after their return remarks that Max Hoffmann "had attended 'Hello, London' in London and had been surprised and gratified, but much more surprised than gratified, to note that the Londoners had appropriated one of his best songs and made it the basis of their play."[41] This surprise illustrates the bilateral flow of influence between European performance and American vaudeville: both continents could be visited, appropriated from, and imitated at a distance.

Gertrude Hoffmann's transatlantic production impersonations exist in a legal gray area; I have tried to give a bit of context about how that gray area functioned within the performance norms of vaudeville in the early twentieth century. Close examination of Hoffmann's work suggests that performance studies scholars need to develop more complex ways for understanding processes of unauthorized cultural borrowing, both historically and as a current practice. As scholars of theatre, we need to be cognizant of the ways that current definitions of intellectual property may shape what we consider to be worthy and unworthy of attention. Instead of being wary of pirates, we need to be more aware of them and the context in which their work is produced, performed, and received.

Notes

1. Zora Neale Hurston, "Characteristics of Negro Expression," in *Sweat*, ed. Cheryl A. Wall (New Brunswick, N.J.: Rutgers University Press, 1997), 55–71.

2. Brian Seibert, *What the Eye Hears: A History of Tap Dancing* (New York: Farrar, Straus and Giroux, 2015); Priya Srinivasan, *Sweating Saris: Indian Dance as Transnational Labor* (Philadelphia: Temple University Press, 2011).

3. Anthea Kraut, *Choreographing Copyright: Race, Gender, and Intellectual Property Rights in American Dance* (Oxford: Oxford University Press, 2015), xii.

4. Hoffmann's life and career have been the sole focus of only two previous articles, both by Barbara Naomi Cohen (now Cohen-Stratyner): "The Borrowed Art of Gertrude Hoffmann," *Dance Data* 2 (1977): 2–11, and "Gertrude Hoffmann: Salome Treads the Boards," *Dance Research Journal* (1978): 23–32.

5. See Cohen, "The Borrowed Art of Gertrude Hoffmann."

6. For a discussion of the Hoffmann Girls from their heyday in the 1920s, see André Levinson, "The Girls," in *André Levinson on Dance: Writings from Paris in the Twenties*, ed. Joan Acocella and Lynn Garafola, trans. Ralph Roeder (Hanover, N.H: Wesleyan University Press, 1991), 89–94.

7. Mary Simonson, *Body Knowledge: Performance, Intermediality, and American Entertainment at the Turn of the Twentieth Century* (Oxford: Oxford University Press, 2013), 34.

8. Robert Spoo, *Without Copyrights: Piracy, Publishing, and the Public Domain* (Oxford: Oxford University Press, 2013), 4.

9. Robinson Locke Collection, *T-Mss 1924–001, Billy Rose Theatre Division, New York Public Library for the Performing Arts, 273:19.

10. Marlis Schweitzer, *Transatlantic Broadway* (New York: Palgrave Macmillan, 2015), loc. 1130 of 6988, http://www.palgraveconnect.com/doifinder/10.1057/9781137437358.

11. "What Greater Vaudeville Promises This Winter: Vaudeville Stars Limited. Europe Scoured for Acts. English Music Hall Standard. Some Klaw & Erlanger Headliners. Keith-Proctor's Big Act's," *New York Times*, September 1, 1907, second magazine section.

12. Spoo, *Without Copyrights*, 50.

13. As I discuss later in the essay, Oscar Hammerstein sent Gertrude Hoffmann to London for exactly this reason.

14. Gertrude Hoffmann, "How the Russian Ballet Was Brought to America," *New York City American*, June 25, 1911, Box 11, Folder 6: Scrapbook with clippings from Russian ballet. Gertrude & Max Hoffmann Papers, Special Collections & Archives, Z. Smith Reynolds Library, Wake Forest University.

15. Elizabeth Kendall, *Where She Danced: The Birth of American Art-Dance* (Berkeley: University of California Press, 1979), 76.

16. Kendall, *Where She Danced*, 84.

17. "Gertrude Hoffmann Dies," *Dance Magazine* 40 (December 1966): 7.

18. Sharyn R. Udall, *Dance and American Art: A Long Embrace* (Madison: University of Wisconsin Press, 2012), 135.

19. For the sake of my argument, I want to emphasize how borrowing and recontextualizing is both part of scholarly discourse and part of Ryle's example cited in Geertz. Ryle's initial use of the term "thick description" takes place in a discussion of several boys engaging in the same physical action (rapidly contracting one eyelid) and how they could be understood as having wholly different messages depending on their intent, audience, and the social codes that they call

upon. Clifford Geertz, *The Interpretation of Cultures: Selected Essays* (New York: Basic Books, 1973), 6–7.

20. Although he is discussing print rather than performance culture, Robert Spoo's monograph restores important context to the discussion of pirated performances as well. He observes that "the typical and uncritical use of the term *piracy*—detached from the legal conditions that permitted and even encouraged it—gives a false aura of illegality to a practice that, though inconsistent with strict business morality…was a lawful form of cultural diffusion well into the twentieth century." Spoo, *Without Copyrights*, 4.

21. Marlis Schweitzer discusses scouting trips to Europe in the wake of the success of *The Merry Widow* in *Transatlantic Broadway: The Infrastructural Politics of Global Performance* (New York: Springer, 2015), Kindle ed. For a discussion of the Pavlova and Mordkin tour and the craze for Russian dancers in their wake, see Suzane Carbonneau Levy, "The Russians Are Coming: Russian Dancers in the United States, 1910–1933," PhD diss., New York University, 1990.

22. Susan A. Glenn, *Female Spectacle: The Theatrical Roots of Modern Feminism* (Cambridge, Mass.: Harvard University Press, 2000), 74–75.

23. For the shift between nineteenth- and twentieth-century American performance, see Julia A. Walker, *Expressionism and Modernism in the American Theatre: Bodies, Voices, Words* (Cambridge: Cambridge University Press, 2005).

24. Marlis Schweitzer, "The Salome Epidemic," in *The Oxford Handbook of Dance and Theater*, ed. Nadine George-Graves (Oxford: Oxford University Press, 2015), 890–921.

25. Schweitzer, "The Salome Epidemic," 911, lists many of the important Salome articles of the past twenty years. In addition to Schweitzer, the two key sources for understanding Hoffmann's appropriations of Maud Allan's dance are Susan A. Glenn, *Female Spectacle: The Theatrical Roots of Modern Feminism* (Cambridge, Mass.: Harvard University Press, 2000), 96–125, and Mary Simonson, *Body Knowledge: Performance, Intermediality, and American Entertainment at the Turn of the Twentieth Century* (Oxford: Oxford University Press, 2013), 27–47.

26. Robinson Locke Collection, 273:19.

27. Simonson, *Body Knowledge*, 33–36.

28. Edward Jewitt Wheeler, "The Vulgarization of Salome," in *Current Literature* 45 (1908): 437–40, at 438.

29. Robinson Locke Collection, 273:24.

30. For proponents of the New Stagecraft in American theatre of the 1910s, "Belascoism" was a dismissive shorthand for the overly detailed realistic stagecraft of producer David Belasco and his imitators. See Sheldon Cheney, The New Movement in the Theatre (New York : M. Kennerley, 1914), 151–76, and Arthur Hopkins, *How's Your Second Act? Notes on the Art of Production* (New York: S. French, 1931).

31. Oliver M. Sayler and Marjorie Barkentin, "On Your Toes—America!: The Story of the First Ballet Russe," *Dance Data* 2 (1977): 20–27, 22.

32. Steven Gary Marks, *How Russia Shaped the Modern World: From Art to*

Anti-Semitism, Ballet to Bolshevism (Princeton, N.J.: Princeton University Press, 2003), 201.

33. Hoffmann, "How the Russian Ballet Was Brought to America."

34. "Display Ad 47—No Title," *New York Times*, June 11, 1911, sec. Drama, X3.

35. "Her exotics were Broadway gypsies; her program employed classical ballet as a form of popular entertainment," says Cohen in "The Borrowed Art of Gertrude Hoffmann."

36. Samuel A. Eliot Jr., "The New Art of the Theater," *Century Illustrated Monthly Magazine*, May 1918, 47.

37. "He dragged us severally to see Gertrude Hoffmann's 'Russian' ballet," notes Hiram Kelly Moderwell in "The Art of Robert Edmond Jones," *Theatre Arts* 1, no. 2 (1917): 51–61, at 52. Note the scare quotes on the word Russian, suggesting that Moderwell too felt the need to dismiss the Hoffmann ballet as inauthentic.

38. Marks, *How Russia Shaped the Modern World*, 201.

39. Schweitzer, *Transatlantic Broadway*, 3330 of 6988.

40. See Peggy Phelan, *Unmarked: The Politics of Performance* (New York: Psychology Press, 1993).

41. Robinson Locke Collection, 273:69.

Greasing the Global

Princess Lotus Blossom and the Fabrication of the "Orient" to Pitch Products in the American Medicine Show

Chase Bringardner

> It was a swashbuckling world, peopled by a few geniuses and a great many rascals. It was a world in which the romance of the four corners of the world could be found in the flame of the pitchman's gasoline torch. The torches are gone, but the names they led to fame are not.
> —Violet McNeal, *Four White Horses and a Brass Band*

In her 1947 autobiography, dramatically entitled *Four White Horses and a Brass Band*, Violet McNeal recounts her days as the premiere female pitch doctor on the medicine show circuit. She describes her journeys throughout the United States in great detail, dotting the countryside with her fellow performers, a wooden wagon, and an endless supply of medicinal cures for a multitude of common ailments. On the medicine show circuit, McNeal most often portrayed a character by the name of Princess Lotus Blossom, a visitor from the Far East well versed in Chinese remedies and cure-alls. Throughout the book, she recounts the development of this character from its initial beginnings at the hands of her "mentor" and husband Will Cooper, to its first appearance on the medicine show stage, to its final performances and subsequent retirement. To further supplement the character of Princess Lotus Blossom, McNeal and her associates also devised elaborate stories to impress audiences and convince them of the wonders of Tiger Fat salve, Vital Sparks, or other vaguely "Oriental" products. Taken together, the character and the stories created an elaborate performance designed to create the maximum amount of wonder and the appropriate amount of exoticism to sell the optimum amount of product.

The underlying culture of the medicine show visible just beneath the surface of these elaborate performances, and McNeal's navigation of that often rough terrain reveals a rich and complicated interplay of the global with gender and racial identity. McNeal's performance of "yellow face," or the donning of makeup and other facial prosthetics to appear "Asian," through the character of Princess Lotus Blossom, for example, facilitates and fosters the commercial and capitalist system of the medicine show—popular theatre used fundamentally to sell products—and illustrates how those concerns influenced her performance decisions. McNeal's gender in a predominately male, hierarchically structured performance tradition informed her decision to portray Asian characters onstage. Performing during a time of increased immigration from China and Japan, McNeal engaged with prevalent stereotypes that labeled Asian immigrants as interlopers, vagabonds, thieves, sexual objects, and opium addicts. These stereotypes contributed to and strengthened Orientalist fantasies that objectified the Asian immigrant and transformed people into products for commercial means. McNeal's performance directly reflects and borrows from this historical and cultural moment. Drawing from McNeal's own account of the process of developing and staging the character of Princess Lotus Blossom, I examine how, at the site of medicine show performance, McNeal's gender, race, and class identities operated through her "yellow face" performance. McNeal's character, Princess Lotus Blossom, revealed the struggle between capitalist and commercial endeavors of the form while simultaneously exhibiting the supposed freedoms, rites, and opportunities that performance afforded her over the "typical" woman of the late nineteenth and early twentieth centuries. I am chiefly concerned with letting Violet McNeal speak through the vivid passages of her autobiography. The male-dominated medicine show culture often silenced female participants, and thus a focus on McNeal's own account serves as an intervention in this patriarchal history. Documenting and decoding McNeal's experiences as expressed in her life work privileges her knowledge over the power structures and forms that often dictated her everyday practice.

The evolution of McNeal's Princess Lotus Blossom must be understood within the context of the often-overlooked popular form and performance culture of the medicine show itself. Medicine shows traveled throughout both North and South and brought urban ideas and practices, such as sophisticated advertising campaigns and increased standards of cleanliness, to rural areas throughout the United States. Like the modern-day late-night television infomercial, medicine shows used performance as a means to sell a variety of quasi-medicinal products and drew from a variety of popular performance traditions, such as minstrelsy, vaudeville, and burlesque.[1] Medicine show performers erected small wooden stages in the center of town, often an extension of the carts on which they rode, where they would stage their pitches for products like Kickapoo Indian Remedy, Snake Oil, or Women's Friend. They presented characters that relied on a shared understanding of regional stereotypes and theatrical stock characters such as the Noble Savage, the "carrot-topped rustic," and various other minstrel characters.[2] In addition to these more formal pitches, medicine shows also offered evenings of performance as further enticement to purchase their products. Underneath large canvas tents similar to those of the Christian revival or early circus, medicine show performers presented evenings of variety performance comprised of skits, audience contests (like the ever-popular female nail-driving competition or sawing contests), and local talent competitions. Audiences actively engaged with these performances through both physical and financial participation.[3]

The American medicine show, and more specifically McNeal's Princess Lotus Blossom, also emerged explicitly from a historical moment preoccupied with the Orient and Orientalism. The word "Oriental," often used in opposition to the term Occidental, signifies the exoticized, commodified, mysterious, and imaginary image of the Far East encouraged in late nineteenth- and early twentieth-century art, literature, fashion, and other popular culture forms. Yet as Edward Said critically reminds in *Orientalism*, the book's namesake exceeds simple classification and rather exists as "a discourse that is by no means in direct, corresponding relationship with political power in the raw, but rather is produced and exists in an uneven exchange with various kinds of power, shaped to a degree by the exchange with political power (as with colonial or imperial establishment), power intellectual (as with reigning sciences like comparative linguistics or anatomy, or modern policy science), power cultural (as with orthodoxies and canons of taste, texts, and values), and power moral (as with ideas about what 'we' do and what 'they' cannot do or understand as 'we' do)."[4] In other words, Orientalism "is a cultural and political fact,"[5] bringing together a cacophony of different forces within the material representation. As a practice, Orientalism leads to a conflation of multiple Asian identities into a vague, generalized, and surface "Oriental" representation that flattens, simplifies, and materializes the Other for easier containment and greater control.[6] As Said states, "Orientalism depends for its strategy on this flexible positional superiority, which puts the Westerner in a whole series of possible relationships with the Orient without ever losing him the relative upper hand."[7]

Material culture of the late nineteenth and early twentieth centuries reveals the impact of Orientalism on the perception and portrayal of Asian Americans. While Asian men typically found themselves relegated to the periphery, rendered powerless and impotent in servitude or opium dens, Asian females usually fell into the category of the overly aggressive, potentially deadly Dragon Woman or the overly passive, sexually alluring, achingly subservient geisha-type. Each stereotype, found in art, fashion, literature, radio, film, and other cultural products, reflected the complex discourse of Orientalism and demonstrated how representation reveals the cultural and the political.

McNeal's medicine show persona directly engaged such Orientalist discourse, using the image of a commodified, sanitized Orient to generate drama and allure in order to pitch and sell fake medicinal products. As Thomas LeBlanc in his 1925 article stated: "The medicine show was the one breath of romance, the one touch of lands across the sea that invaded the isolation of our remote little town."[8] Violet McNeal's "romance" with the medicine show began in Minnesota at the end of the nineteenth century with a secretarial job and a man named Will. McNeal, in her autobiography, describes her journey from economic hardship, in a bedbug-ridden tenement in a small town outside of St. Paul to the height of popularity on the medicine show circuit. After successfully escaping the stifling, economically deprived conditions of her childhood, McNeal arrived in the big city of St. Paul and witnessed her first theatrical entertainment, presumably some sort of burlesque show or extravaganza. Once she got over her initial horror at the women "naked, except for a little skirt and some little things over their breasts," she gradually came to embrace theatrical performance primarily as a means of making money without really working.[9] After failed attempts at a secretarial career, she determined that "only suckers work."[10] Luckily her boss at the time, Will McNeal, took more than a passing interest in her and got her involved in the production and marketing of a new medicinal cure. As he taught her the tools of the trade, she fell in love: "He talked to me about what I thought about marriage, love, the Bible, and other subjects. He was the first person who ever had been interested in my opinions."[11] McNeal described him as a direct departure from the rural boys she was used to: "He was always clean-shaven, his hair had a nice smell. His fingers were slender and deft."[12] In essence, Will had taken a page directly out of the medicine show handbook and given Violet the hard sell, which she bought wholeheartedly.

Violet and Will were married and her "education" continued. As Violet remembers vividly, "He talked to me by the hour...about Confucius, Buddha, and Mohammed."[13] Yet Violet got more than she bargained for when Will's affections turned violent. Will frequently lost his temper with Violet, knocking her out on numerous occasions and sending her to the hospital more than a few times. Will's physical violence became an enduring marker and metaphor for Violet's struggles against the male-dominated world of the medicine show. She quickly realized that Will called the shots in their marriage—"I am your husband and I know what is best for you"—and that if she stepped out of line, emotional and physical brutality would soon follow.[14] The mounting incidents of abuse, coupled with his "educational" talks of distant lands and adventure combined with her desire to rise above her meager economic conditions, led McNeal to dream of far-off places. After attending the St. Louis World's Fair, Violet, inspired and empowered by the infinite possibilities she encountered there, and with a consenting Will by her side, decided not to return home to Minnesota and instead traveled to Oklahoma City. Once there, at the urging of her husband, "a curly-haired man" taught Violet "a mind-reading act—a little one—twenty-six articles on the alphabet code."[15] Will encouraged the development of his wife's new skills and saw her talents as a way of supplementing both their life on the road and his own developing drug habits. As her skill increased, Violet immersed herself more and more within the itinerant, popular entertainment community and eventually formed relationships with established medicine men, collecting valuable knowledge and techniques. These medicine men became her "idols."[16] McNeal's fascination with medicine shows led directly to her and her husband's decision that she would become a pitchwoman, at which point Will sat Violet down at the young age of seventeen and told her what and who she would become: Princess Lotus Blossom.

McNeal and Will interacted forcefully with Orientalist discourse when they went about selecting their initial medicine show personas. Medicine shows traditionally drew from decidedly American native types to create characters for their pitches and skits: "the American Indian—sometimes real but usually fake; the cowboy, dressed like Buffalo Bill; the Midwestern farm boy seen as a freckled face Toby; and the sober, honest Quaker."[17] However, McNeal and Will found inspiration in late nineteenth- and early twentieth-century Orientalist constructions. Inspired by time spent in San Francisco and other cities with sizable Chinese immigrant communities, McNeal and Will crafted an Orientalist fantasy from the memories of their own personal experiences. A long-time opium addict, Will chiefly drew inspiration from a number of "Chinese doctors" with whom he frequently smoked. Having created his own Chinese persona to sell Chinese headache oil, Will "was from then on identified with things Chinese, and his warmest personal interests centered on the subject."[18] Violet recalls that Will frequently told her tales of the Chinese heroes of history and, in fact, eventually forced her, by threat of beating, to begin smoking opium. Whenever their journeys took them to a major city, they would travel into the area known as Chinatown looking for the latest imported rarity or oddity like dried lizard, bamboo, or small clumps of dried herbs "in their natural state" called "blood balls."[19]

As a matter of course, Princess Lotus Blossom grew out of Will's fascination with the Orient that he forced upon Violet. His initial foray into the medicine show profession came via Dr. Lop Chung, a father figure who purportedly encouraged Will to construct a Chinese character for himself. Chung urged Will to appropriate Chinese culture and cultivate pitches that relied on Orientalist discourse. A 1961 issue of *Harper's Magazine* recalls similar instructions given to some pitch doctors: "For a more artful kind of soap merchandising you go to a Chinese laundry and promote an old newspaper, to use for wrapping with the ends twisted like candy wrapper. Now you go out in the street, 'build a tip,' and explain that this is imported Chinese Corn Punk."[20] Fellow opium addict Dr. Chung, "a tall, dignified Chinese who spoke English perfectly," likewise encouraged McNeal's participation and bestowed upon her a kimono[21] "of ivory satin, embroidered on one side with pink cherry blossoms, and on the other with white cherry blossoms against a pale pink background."[22] When the time came for Violet's transformation into a pitch doctor, a Chinese woman seemed the natural choice—an exotic character that appealed to potential rural audiences desiring the mysterious and foreign, to Will's drug-addled visions, and to Violet herself. Fortuitously, Violet found a kindred spirit in Madame du Bois, the first woman to create and produce her own medicine show. Du Bois along with her husband, Dr. Andrew Dupre, had established themselves as the premiere practitioners of painless tooth pulling. Upon Madame du Bois's death, she was believed to have been worth nearly a million dollars.[23] The prospect of immense wealth, spectacular fame, and financial independence led McNeal to begin developing her own Princess Lotus Blossom pitches and to declare herself formally the heir apparent to du Bois.[24]

McNeal's first pitch for a salve called Tiger Fat relied heavily on her labor, both physical labor onstage and domestic labor offstage, although the latter remained invisible to the consuming public. Not yet an established pitchwoman, McNeal produced her Tiger Fat remedies "in whatever hotel or rooming house the couple made their headquarters."[25] The process of creating the salve mirrored typical domestic tasks, even involving a few similar ingredients: "We melted the Vaseline in a large bucket over a gas jet, adding gun camphor, menthol crystals, oil of eucalyptus, turpentine, and oil of wintergreen…then stirred it briskly."[26] Yet this domesticity took place offstage and therefore did little to bolster Violet's onstage persona. Ironically (or perhaps not surprisingly for her time period), her dreams of wealth and fame remained, at least at first, explicitly tied to the same invisible domestic labor she sought to escape. Yet her onstage performance afforded more potential opportunities for McNeal to establish herself and make her mark.

Onstage, McNeal transformed into Princess Lotus Blossom, "a short, slim, and very pretty Chinese girl."[27] Instead of emphasizing her domesticity, the character of Lotus Blossom capitalized on her beauty and mysterious charm. Stewart Holbrook in *The Golden Age of Quackery* remarked that after seeing a photograph of McNeal as Lotus Blossom he "began to understand how she had managed to survive three busy decades in a racket dominated by and comprised almost wholly of men."[28] McNeal constructed a beautiful, exotic, and, most importantly, safe feminine ideal for her audiences while simultaneously, backstage, maintaining a hidden, strong domestic sensibility. In many ways, this initial pitch only reified traditional gender roles because McNeal's labor remained (albeit necessarily) hidden behind a curtain, a pretty face, and a simplistic story of a Chinese physician who cut up a tiger to create this wondrous salve. Yet this pitch also revealed an important complexity and ambiguity through the duality of her performance of "Orientalist" attitudes of both the domestic and the exotic. Moreover, the pitch highlighted McNeal's limited control over the performance and gestured toward possible subversion that her later pitches would exhibit.

Determined to deepen her impact and sharpen her technique, McNeal modified the character of Princess Lotus Blossom in her second pitch for Vital Sparks, an impotence cure, and offered a more nuanced performance. While she maintained her beauty and exoticism, she also displayed an "excellent voice," "good English," intelligence, and "quiet eloquence" and performed with "an unusual bell-like contralto"—all measures meant to "Americanize" and further contain her Asian persona.[29] Unlike the brash, loud style of most medicine men, McNeal opted for a more subtle approach using a combination of traditionally female gendered characteristics, for example using soft vocal inflection and gentle hand gestures to appear coy, to create a complex composite of a woman still suitable to an audience of prospective, proper consumers.

Despite her reliance on mostly traditional gendered, stereotypically passive Asian characteristics and gestures—placing both hands to the mouth to cover quiet laughter and continually bowing the head slightly—McNeal did find moments of subversion. For instance, at one point in the pitch "it was Lady Blossom's custom to pause again, and briefly to sweep her audience with one quick bold challenging look; and then, as if startled by so unladylike an action in herself, instantly drop her eyes in a convincing try for girlish confusion."[30] Here, McNeal directly confronts the audience, disrupting the moment of performance and inviting them fleetingly behind the carefully constructed façade. The stark juxtaposition of this unorthodox glare with the subsequent moment of feigned confusion may have reminded the audience of the artificiality of performance and that they were watching an act. This moment might also gesture to the dragon lady lurking inside McNeal's Orientalist creation or to the complicated nature of Orientalist female representation itself. The glare's simultaneous physical specificity and ambiguous meaning highlight the power of performance to create interpretive space and disrupt conventions. The quick gesture to artifice likewise calls attention to the performance of gender while simultaneously demonstrating McNeal's command as a performer. In that moment of distance between performer and character, the audience might then have considered this disconnect and realized the multiple performances occurring simultaneously (Asian woman, Blossom, medicine woman, McNeal). Even if the audience did not make the connection, McNeal's aggressive "wink" to the audience demonstrates her own acknowledgment of the multiple layers and potential meanings of her performance. The brief glimpse behind the curtain highlights the constructed nature of the performance and perhaps even reminds the audience that they play a role as well and will soon be invited to enact their own character through purchasing the product.

Furthermore, the product itself, Vital Sparks, positioned McNeal and her performance of race in an interesting manner, and provided other potential moments of subversion. McNeal, a white woman dressed in yellow-face and Orientalist attire, labored to sell a cure for impotence within a stereotypical racial context that purposely de-emphasized Asian masculinity in an attempt to control it. The character of Lotus Blossom was both a potential savior for the afflicted and a reminder of their inadequacies—the "Asian" female body that the impotent (Asian) man could not satisfy. Yet for a predominantly white audience, her female "Asian" body allowed white men to displace their fears of impotency onto the cultural construct of the Asian man, her natural counterpart, and read her within a colonial discourse of possession and domination.

It would appear that McNeal and Will intentionally constructed the story of the pitch in an attempt to appease this tension (and in turn the male audience). In the story, the people of China are saved from potential ruin due to a decline in the birth rate by a remedy made from the "brain pouch" of male turtles.[31] As Will instructed McNeal to pronounce in her act: "At one time in China, you will say, the people lost most of their virility. The birth rate was so low, and family life was disintegrating. So the Emperor issued a proclamation offering a reward the equivalent of ten thousand dollars to the person who would make a discovery capable of restoring their normal vitality to the people."[32] Despite the best efforts of doctors and scientists, no one could find a cure until He Tuck Chaw came upon "countless thousands of small turtlelike animals" while exploring "in the volcanic region."[33] Through observation Chaw noted that for every one male turtle there appeared to be nearly one thousand female turtles. Feeling certain he was near a scientific breakthrough, Chaw dissected one of the male turtles and discovered that "it possessed a small pouch at the base of its brain," the "Quali Quah pouch."[34] As Will's concocted story continued: "He removed the pouches from the male animals, dried and powdered them, and gave tiny portions to the Chinese people. Their reaction was both swift and effective. He Tuck Chaw was loaded with honors and money. There is, gentlemen, a sufficient quantity of this same substance in these Vital Sparks I am going to offer tonight to restore your health, virility, and happiness."[35] McNeal in her pitch thus aligned impotence not explicitly with sexual malfunction but with an inability to procreate—using the Chinese male as an ideal surrogate in the story for the struggling American man—and locating the cure within the male species (of turtle) itself. Not only would Vital Sparks "restore your health, virility, and happiness,"[36] but it would also apparently increase virility as that one male turtle could service nearly one thousand female turtles! This positioning of the story skillfully allowed the American male to displace his impotency onto the Asian man, shifting the discussion away from American male sexuality and into the realm of an Orientalist fantastical sphere.

While Vital Sparks provided McNeal with newfound popularity and vitality, these successes, perhaps ironically, challenged Will's power and prowess. As a result, his resentment and control increased. Drawn into the dark void of a life of drugs, alcohol, and gambling, Will often took his frustrations out on Violet. After one particularly harrowing night in which Violet threatened divorce, Will expressed his desire to have her tonsils removed, a procedure she was much in need of due to persistent sore throats. She relates the incident: "The next morning the doctor came and I was given ether. When I came to I was in bed in the next room, and Will was sitting beside me. My throat wasn't sore, but the whole of one leg above the knee was paining me terribly. Will leaned over my face. 'You dirty, chippy slut! You thought you could leave me, did you? You damned ungrateful little tramp, you thought you could ditch me after all I've done for you!' He tore the bedcovers back. 'Look at that!' I looked; I screamed; I nearly fainted. A large Chinese dragon was tattooed on my left thigh. I closed my eyes. 'You're branded as mine as long as you live,' Will said. 'I'm going to have a dragon tattooed on my forearm tomorrow. We'll go to our graves marked the same.'"[37] Through this action, Will branded Violet with a permanent reminder of his Orientalist Asian fascination, literally and metaphorically scarring her with the mark of Asian representation he had encouraged her years before to pursue. To appease his guilt, he insisted on lavishing Violet with gifts like furs, jewelry, and even "a Japanese cook and a maid."[38] Paradoxically, of course, these purchases were made with Violet's own earnings. Shortly after learning that Will was, in fact, already married, and after procuring a suitable, stable male replacement to assure her continued financial stability, Violet filed for divorce from Will and in doing so freed herself not just from a highly abusive relationship but from the character of Princess Lotus Blossom.

Violet, though violently and forcefully drawn to the Orient through Will's destructive obsession, came to see the character of Princess Lotus Blossom as a way to rise above her class position, to achieve financial success, to actively partake in the capitalist system, and to transcend white female respectability. Through the construction of Princess Lotus Blossom, Violet and Will participated in the commodification of the Orient popular in the United States in the late nineteenth and early twentieth centuries. McNeal's performance, like Said's many examples of literature and art in *Orientalism*, confirmed "the continuing imperial design to dominate Asia."[39] Staging the Asian female body in performance, as Karen Shimakawa notes in *National Abjection: The Asian American Body Onstage*, contained the "threat to the (literal and symbolic) 'American body' by the immigrant body."[40] Possessing and controlling the image in performance provided Violet a certain imperial power reserved for those identified as white and almost always male. Her use of the "Orient" not only increased the drama but also applied to this popular entertainment the late nineteenth- and early twentieth-century ideals of colonialism, imperialism, and containment that attempted to conquer, control, and possess the Far East. In the medicine show, Orientalism offered McNeal a potential pathway to great fortune.

Yet Violet sought more than mere financial success. She sought freedom from the confines of her husband's often tyrannical rule, as well as the life of adventure and excitement promised in stories that Will had told her when she fell in love with him. Living alongside medicine show companies, she discovered that the wives of the medicine men, although "lovely ladies, bejeweled and beautifully dressed," did not "make much [of] an impression" because "they weren't spectacular."[41] In other words, they did not emerge from the shadows of their husbands. This observation from her autobiography illustrates McNeal's desire to step outside of traditional gender boundaries to assume a more visible position. Not content to remain in the shadows with the wives of the medicine men or her own husband, she wanted more. Furthermore, escalating violence in her marriage left Violet struggling to find a means of supporting herself outside of Will's often-volatile grip. Performance provided McNeal the opportunity to live a life outside of Minnesota, escape her stifling marriage, and lead a life of adventure on the road.

Princess Lotus Blossom afforded McNeal a vehicle to engage in a medicine show performance culture antithetical to traditional white womanhood. As Richard Dyer states in *White*, "White women thus carry…the hopes, achievements, and character of the race" and thusly find themselves beholden to societal expectations that contain and restrict.[42] Ironically, McNeal escaped (at least temporarily while on stage) the confines of her white womanhood through the enactment of a contained image of the "other." The initial pitch Will provided her with emphasized Princess Lotus Blossom's royal lineage while simultaneously limiting any implied power by making her the offspring of "a Scotch missionary doctor and a Chinese princess."[43] Locating her Chinese ancestry in the matrilineal line and emphasizing her partial Western roots lessened the threat that Princess Lotus Blossom might turn out to be a conniving, deadly Dragon Lady and allowed her to remain a passive vessel. Yet even within this passive construction, McNeal remained a subversive figure pushing against the boundaries of her gender and frequently exceeding its confines. She claimed economic and commercial power, manufacturing and providing her own supplies and pitching the product herself onstage at a time when most women generally remained relegated to the role of consumer. Through her own performance of Asian femininity, Violet managed the potential risk of the Asian body and in doing so assured herself a place within and outside both the patriarchal-capitalist system and the larger male-dominated American ethos.

As a medicine woman, McNeal used her femininity and her whiteness to her advantage. She skillfully alternated between conforming to traditional gender roles and breaking out of them. Unlike her predecessor du Bois, McNeal reversed the traditional gendered husband-wife relationship commonly found within medicine shows by performing alone, without her husband, who preferred a role behind the scenes, smoking opium and gambling. The sight of her female body alone onstage, simultaneously reading as white and "other" as a result of the yellow-face makeup, signified something quite unusual to audiences. An anomaly on the medicine-show stage, the solo female presence presented a potentially risky proposition, an unstable signifier, not easily quantified or understood, with a narrative in need of completion. While the narrative of the medicine show pitch concluded with the purchase of the product, McNeal's

Princess Lotus Blossom herself defied resolution, manipulating that intrigue and mystery to sell more goods. The solo female performer costumed as an exotic Asian character moreover presented an image of the "Orient" ripe for possession and control by men (and perhaps women) in the audience. The pitch conflated the act of purchase with the act of cultural appropriation. To buy the product allowed the audience member to purchase a piece of the "Orient." With each new pitch she developed, McNeal incorporated a variety of theatrical techniques and gendered and racial performances ultimately geared to make the sale. Even though the goal of the medicine show was to sell a product, her shifting bodily performances disrupted the common construction of the female body as commodity and shifted it onto an Asian one, thus dislocating dominant gender discourse and creating space, through performance, for disruption.

McNeal's performances as Princess Lotus Blossom on the medicine show stage rehearsed her eventual discovery of her own power. After leaving Will and thus liberating herself not only from his domination but also from his fixation on Asian culture, Violet fashioned a new character. This newfound freedom—psychologically and socially, if not economically—led to McNeal's most obviously subversive gender display with her final pitch for "Pure Concentrate of Madame V. Pasteur's Herbs."[44] As with the Tiger Fat and Vital Sparks, she concocted the mixture on her own, yet this time a medicine manufacturer took over subsequent production. Instead of Princess Lotus Blossom and her performance of Asian femininity, McNeal created the new character of Madame V. Pasteur, a deliberate reference to Louis Pasteur, dressed in fitted academic robe and mortarboard. Madame Pasteur was a scientist, and the pitch included numerous "scientific" demonstrations and tests. By incorporating science into her pitch, McNeal defied the traditionally limited roles of women at the turn of the century. Most overtly, she included within her pitch a "masterful tribute to Great Women, speaking well and easily of Elizabeth of England, Catherine of Russia, Isabella of Spain; then shifted to Helena Blavatsky and Annie Besant. She had good words for Sarah Bernhardt too."[45] McNeal reserved her highest accolades, though, for Madame Curie. In this moment, she commented directly on her own now-defunct marriage, celebrating Madame Curie's contributions to science while downplaying Monsieur Curie and essentially blaming him for the accident that cost them their lives.[46] McNeal made no direct linkages between these women and the product, presumably leaving a gap in meaning for the audience to fill. The celebration of these women as independent agents not directly tied to the products pitched created an atmosphere where to purchase the product perhaps allowed the buyer to put on and embody the traits of these great women. The act of purchasing the concentrate held within it a possibly political action, though couched in the language of domestic consumerism. This gesture toward reclaiming women historical figures to sell, albeit indirectly, an herbal concentrate illustrates the often complicated, often exciting nature of the medicine show and McNeal's skillful ability to exploit the multiple layers of meaning often occurring simultaneously.

The strange life and career of Violet McNeal illustrates a complicated interplay of race, gender, and class within the culture of the medicine show. Violet, through the performance of Princess Lotus Blossom, took advantage of national fears of increasing Asian presence in the United States and offered a performance of containment that packaged Orientalism in an attractive commercial interaction and abetted fears of the perceived Asian threat. Through purchasing a salve or remedy, consumers could do their part to squelch the danger of this new immigrant population (literally to put "them" in their place on the shelf). For Violet, the performance allowed her to rise above precarious, meager economic conditions and establish herself as a powerful businesswoman creating her own pitches and products during a time when few women were afforded such privileges in a male-dominated, capitalist society. Violet's appropriation of Asian stereotypes to achieve power, financial success, and eventual personal freedom speaks to the complex interplay between race and gender and culture that occurred in many early American popular entertainment forms. This reclaiming of the life of Violet McNeal through her own words illustrates this complicated relationship and speaks to the difficult decisions she made both in performance and in life to achieve her hopes and dreams. In the end, despite attempts to distance herself from the Princess Lotus Blossom character, the mark of her previous racist performance remained. Like the indelible tattoo Will had etched into her thigh, the image of Princess Lotus Blossom endured, hidden ironically under the academic robes that adorned her new character.

Notes

1. The modern infomercial draws heavily from the tradition of the medicine show combining product demonstrations and testimonials with theatrical and performance elements to create a spectacle around a given product. While these infomercials do not explicitly embody practices of minstrelsy, vaudeville, or other popular forms, implicit traces remain in the over-the-top delivery, incorporation of music, and reliance on performance narrative.

2. The medicine show borrowed frequently and liberally from the minstrel

show, populating its skits and musical performances with stereotypical characters such as Sambo and Mammy.

3. Brooks McNamara, *Step Right Up: Revised Edition* (Jackson: University Press of Mississippi, 1995).

4. Edward Said, *Orientalism* (New York: Vintage Books, 1979), 12.

5. Ibid., 13.

6. Even though contemporary critical discourse often prefers the use of the word "Asian," much new scholarship points to the potential problems with using such a term. "Asian" potentially reifies many of the concerns with the word "Oriental" in that it also conflates numerous identities under a blanket, overly simplistic term.

7. Said, *Orientalism*, 7.

8. Thomas J. LeBlanc, "The Medicine Show," *American Mercury* 5 (June 1925): 18, 235.

9. Violet McNeal, *Four White Horses and a Brass Band* (New York: Doubleday & Company 1947), 7.

10. Ibid., 18.

11. Ibid., 13.

12. Ibid., 14.

13. Ibid., 16.

14. Ibid., 21.

15. Ibid., 23.

16. Ibid., 70.

17. Paul Wagner and Steven J. Zeitlin, "Free Show Tonight," May 3, 2006, Folkstreams.net.

18. McNeal, *Four White Horses*, 34.

19. Ibid., 151.

20. Long John Nebel, "The Pitchman." *Harper's Magazine* 222 (May 1961): 1332, 52.

21. McNeal's use of a kimono, a traditional Japanese garment, in the creation of a decidedly Chinese character illustrates the slippage and conflation often found in Orientalist discourse.

22. McNeal, *Four White Horses*, 20.

23. Ibid., 72.

24. McNamara, *Step Right Up*, 32.

25. Stewart H. Holbrook, *The Golden Age of Quackery* (New York: Macmillan, 1959), 187.

26. Ibid.

27. Ibid., 189.

28. Ibid.

29. Ibid., 188–89, 191.

30. Ibid., 190.

31. Ibid.

32. McNeal, *Four White Horses*, 74.

33. Ibid.

34. Ibid.

35. Ibid.

36. Ibid.

37. Ibid., 204.

38. Ibid., 131.

39. Said, *Orientalism*, 322.

40. Karen Shimakawa, *National Abjection: The Asian American Body Onstage.* (Durham, N.C.: Duke University Press, 2002), 7.

41. McNeal, *Four White Horses*, 71.

42. Richard Dyer, *White* (New York: Routledge, 1997), 29.

43. McNeal, *Four White Horses*, 73.

44. Holbrook, *The Golden Age of Quackery*, 192.

45. Ibid., 193–94.

46. Ibid., 194.

Dismembering Tennessee Williams

The Global Context of Lee Breuer's
A Streetcar Named Desire

Daniel Ciba

Over the past sixty years, Tennessee Williams has become one of the most widely produced playwrights worldwide; his works have been translated into many languages, and he is considered by some to be the American Shakespeare.[1] As new productions reinterpret the meanings of *A Streetcar Named Desire*, directors, actors, critics, and audiences attempt to answer questions about the global significance of Williams's most canonical text. Contemporary critics' resistance to and dismissal of Ivo van Hove's *Streetcar* (1999), deconstructed around a bathtub, confirms a culturally constructed "true" interpretation, generally agreed on by American critics, which firmly locates the text as realistic, performed by realistic characters, and set in a realistic New Orleans.[2] Lee Breuer's production of *Streetcar*, performed at the Comédie Française in Paris in 2011, serves as an example of the complicated politics underlying productions of *Streetcar* that eschew the realism now associated with the original production and the subsequent film, both directed by Elia Kazan. Reading Breuer's production as an example of cross-cultural dialogue on the global stage, I intend to adapt the concept of "counter-memories" as theorized by Michel Foucault to accentuate the distance between Breuer's nonrealistic global contextualization of the play from memories of Kazan's "realistic" American contexts.

In an essay investigating the concept of genealogy via the philosophies of Nietzsche, Foucault develops the term "counter-memory" as a means of discussing the differences between history and reality. To Foucault, counter-memory illustrates an opposition to the monolithic construct of history, which supports the institutionalization of discourse surrounding an author. Foucault claims that the vast difference between constructed history and its counter-memory is a historiographical issue: "We want historians to confirm our belief that the present rests upon profound intentions and immutable necessities. But the true historical sense confirms our existence among countless lost events, without a landmark or point of reference."[3] According to Foucault, when considering the sum of an author's work, there exists a dominant history that is assumed to be true, but there also exists a counter-memory that runs counter to that dominant history. Foucault notes that these oppositions "imply a use of history that severs its connection to memory, its metaphysical and anthropological model, and constructs a counter-memory—a transformation of history into a totally different form of time."[4] By transforming the temporality of history, Foucault seeks to recover Nietzsche's ideas from cultural inscription.

Counter-memory, as Foucault describes it, offers an opportunity for historians and critics to escape ideologies that only communicate dominant hegemony. In this analysis, I define counter-memories as disruptions to the culturally inscribed hegemonic reading of a production history. Because *Streetcar* has entered the American canon as an example of the now globally transmitted institution of American realism, Williams has achieved the status that Foucault attributes to Nietzsche. Williams's works function not only as individual texts that can be interpreted in numerous ways and performed in numerous styles, but also, collectively, as an ideological discourse. In order to adapt Foucault's discursive concept into a practical method for this production history, I assume that much of what has been written about Kazan's production conveys the ideological flaw that Foucault identifies with history. I read moments from Breuer's production as counter-memories to dismember the hegemonic cultural memories surrounding Kazan's production and more thoroughly analyze the global elements beyond a simple comparison to Kazan's.

Dismemberment, in relation to the global conversation inherent in Breuer's production, means more than a metaphorical ripping apart of the normative memories surrounding Williams's corpus, especially as they are remembered as sites of institutionalized American realism. I use the verb "dismember" to represent terms employed in my examination of Breuer's production that emphasize the process of remembering beyond the normative concepts typically evoked by production histories. Thus "dismember" becomes an umbrella term for all of the processes derived from my reconsideration of these counter-memories. Although I do not always use the verb dismember, mainly for the sake of variation, my non-normative inscription of each memory of Breuer's production is fueled by the goal of dis-membering, which could also be expressed as dis-remembering, de-constructing the memory, or forgetting the inscribed normative assessment of Williams, for which I use verbs such as disrupt, disconnect, and delocalize.

Dismembering is different from, but not oppositional to, remembering. My analysis of Breuer's production allows for a conceptualization of this new form of production history, focused entirely on reading embodied memories from the current production against culturally inscribed normative memories of the original. Dismembering also allows this new form of construction to accentuate the global conversation in ways that a traditional production history does not. Through my analysis, I describe these counter-memories in order to highlight the global discussion within elements of Breuer's production, referring to this entire process as dismembering.

Such dismemberment of the hegemony surrounding the original production of *Streetcar* might allow current nontraditional productions to avoid critical dismissal. Directed by Elia Kazan, the 1947 Broadway production was labeled by Harold Clurman as "the triumph of Stanley with the collusion of the audience."[5] What Clurman proposed as a misreading of the text—which contradicts Williams's communications with Kazan that "There are no 'good' or 'bad' people in the play"—has over time become part of how scholars, such as Nancy Tischler, read the text:[6] "We know that [Stanley] is the one adapted to the twentieth century. Like the imagery in *The Glass Menagerie*, we see that electricity is replacing candles, that realism is trumping romanticism. Blanche may insist that the poker party is nothing but a gathering of apes, but we realize that it is also the image of twentieth-century man—seven-card stud. Her brand of gentility has been dealt out."[7] Although Tischler complicates this reading with feminist and queer revisions, the male Stanley represents reality and the female Blanche represents illusion. In "A Streetcar Named Misogyny," Kathleen Margaret Lant critiques the misogyny that this culturally inscribed, hegemonic reading implies. Lant considers the implications of Stanley's rape of Blanche as her victimization, relying on stabilized gender roles that interpret male symbols as dominant and female symbols as oppressed.[8] In other words, a simplification of the hegemonic reading of Kazan's production makes Stanley the winner because he lives in a real male world of truth, and Blanche the loser because she creates a fake world built on feminine illusion.

As I use counter-memories to interpret Breuer's production, I rely on the notion that global theatre implies a process of exchange between cultures. Dan Rebellato in *Theater & Globalization* suggests localization and globalization as a false binary.[9] In contrast to his assessment that cosmopolitanism is a potential solution to globalization, I propose delocalization as a strategy, already implicit in Breuer's production, which makes the global relationship among the cultures more apparent. As a newly emerging thesis in the field of economics, Dale Southerton defines delocalization as "the belief that there is an ongoing process whereby the process of making things local is being reversed."[10] In economics, delocalization is considered a negative, a "loss of local cultures (cultural delocalization) due to the advent of a homogenous global culture founded on 'Westernized' or 'Americanized' cultural values."[11] Applying these terms to theatre, I would define localized theatre as implying a real location that contains real characters. In contrast, delocalized theatre would disconnect from a real location, emphasizing a more ambiguous construction of setting and character. By contrasting the negative aspects associated with delocalization, I suggest that delocalization could be a positive and helpful tool to understand what Breuer is doing. In this dismemberment of Breuer's *Streetcar*, I read counter-memories in order to reveal the global cultural elements, by examining delocalization as strategy emerging from Breuer's choices.

In order to reinterpret *Streetcar* for a European audience, Breuer built on his previous strategies of finding avant-garde ways of interpreting canonical texts similar to the way that contemporary directors stage Shakespeare and Chekhov.[12] As a founding member of Mabou Mines, a company dedicated to developing American avant-garde performance, Breuer is a fascinating choice as director for the first American work to enter the repertoire of the Comédie Française.[13] His popular adaptations of Sophocles' *Oedipus at Colonus* and Ibsen's *A Doll House* demonstrated Breuer's penchant for rethinking canonical texts within contemporary contexts. With *Gospel at Colonus* Breuer juxtaposed black gospel music with religious elements of the source material, drawing Christian parallels to Greek mythology by staging the performance as if it were a church service.[14] In *Dollhouse*, the significant height differences between the male and female actors created a physical means of demonstrating the inequality of the female characters, exaggerated by having a three-foot Torvald dominate a six-foot Nora.[15] In both of these productions, Breuer interpreted the text in opposition to assumed traditional contexts associated by contemporary scholars with Sophocles and Ibsen. Thus he used counter-memories to decenter these canonical texts.

With *Colonus*, *Dollhouse*, and *Streetcar*, Breuer's avant-garde approach freed these productions from reinscribing hegemony by enabling a conversation among cultures. In a 1989 interview, Breuer discusses the mixture of dramatic conventions in terms of interculturalism, referencing the power dynamic between mainstream and oppressed cultures: "Even though there is a thrust toward interrelationship of cultures, each culture is struggling at the same time, to keep its own sense while being usurped by larger and more powerful cultures....I also feel deeply involved with the side that says culture can be shared, without its power being taken away in the process of exchange."[16] Breuer relied on this thoughtful approach to interculturalism as a process of exchange in staging *Streetcar*. Consequently, the counter-memories I read from Breuer's production reveal a more global consideration, encouraging discussion among different cultures that could replace conventional localized memories.

To illustrate how intercultural counter-memories enable a more global interpretation of Breuer's *Streetcar*, I emphasize three sites of counter-memory: design elements, acting style, and critical reception. For each site, I present the stable memories associated with Kazan's production, disconnect Breuer's interpretation from Kazan's by reading embodied evidence as counter-memories, and then suggest how this process of dismemberment allows for a more global understanding of the new production, not based entirely on the reinscription of American, hegemonically inscribed memories as the correct interpretation from which the later production deviates.[17]

Dismembering the cultural memories inscribed by the original production with embodied counter-memories is a necessary step in order to evaluate Breuer's interpretation beyond both American and normative conventions. Breuer's *Streetcar* is global because it involves multiple cultures. The first culture is American, which originated in Williams's text and Breuer's directing style indicative of the American avant-garde. The second culture is Japanese, contributed by Breuer's use of Japanese dramatic conventions and the integration of Eastern images in the set. The third culture is French, embodied by the French actors and audiences. Breuer wanted to explore *Streetcar* beyond what has now become a canonized, classic interpretation centered entirely on realism and/or localization, as seen here:

> BREUER: But the main point about Kazan and Williams for me is that I've always thought that there was a conflict between Kazan's kind of cinematic realism and Williams's charged realism....I would say that every play has a first staging, and that staging, if the play lasts, becomes the classic interpretation. Then, later on, the play becomes open to new exploration.[18]

Rather than constructing separate, localized settings or characters, Breuer encouraged these three cultures to interact throughout the rehearsals and the performances.

In contrast to Breuer's setting, which emphasized a conversation among different cultures, the setting for Kazan's production was decidedly American. Yet the memories surrounding designs for the original production raise questions of form—the important decision whether to stage the play realistically or expressionistically. As Williams began to re-think traditional conventions of plot and character, he was aware of the importance of setting in his conception of dramatic form. His notes on sets, music, and lighting for *The Glass Menagerie* lay out his thoughts for that play, which lead to what he describes as a "plastic" theatre crafted in opposition to "the straight realistic play with its genuine Frigidaire and authentic ice-cubes."[19] Jo Mielziner, the set and lighting designer for the Broadway premieres of several of Williams's early plays, including *Menagerie*, built his designs for *Streetcar* on the traditions of the nonrealistic New Stagecraft inherited from Appia, Craig, and, directly, his mentor Robert Edmond Jones.[20] By the 1990s, the expressionistic details embodied in Mielziner's designs for *Streetcar*—specifically the transparent scrims and the lighting effects—had been abandoned for productions more focused on realism.[21] Without an expressionistic set, the stage version of *Streetcar* becomes focused on reality rather than memory. Similarly, after decades of cultural inscription, the more concrete reality of the setting captured in the film has displaced Williams's resistance to the conventions of realism and the nonrealistic elements of Mielziner's set.[22] These non-realistic counter-memories that contradict a realistic setting for *Streetcar* support Breuer's choice of a delocalized setting that allows the interaction between different cultures.

Disrupting the assumed reality of *Streetcar*'s setting in the Comédie Française production, Breuer collaborated with his designer, Basil Twist, using Japanese dramatic forms to inspire the sets.[23] Twist, who had previously worked with Breuer on the Japanese-inspired *Red Beads*, employed the conventions of Japanese Bunraku puppet theatre to create a set of screens filled with expressionistic Eastern images.[24] For example, in the moment when Blanche recounts the suicide of her homosexual husband, Allen Grey, Breuer and Twist placed a screen with a young Samurai behind her.[25] As she remembers the moment when Grey killed himself, in Breuer's production the screen switched to reveal the Samurai killing himself with a sword. Japanese forms inspired not only the set in this moment, but also the costumes and props. For instance, Renato Bianchi costumed Blanche in a colorful kimono, an image opposite to Lucinda Ballard's Western pastel costumes for both Jessica Tandy on Broadway and Vivien Leigh in the film.[26] The vibrant colors of Bianchi's designs disrupted the softer and starker tone of Ballard's designs, for audiences who had seen the black-and-white film. In addition, the stagehands for the Comédie Française production, reminiscent of Japanese kurogo, moved stage platforms and handed props to the actors in full view of the audience, creating an even greater sense of the constructed nature of the performance.

The addition of Japanese elements created visual oppositions to more lo-calized/realistic/Americentric interpretations of *Streetcar*'s setting.

When asked in an interview about the stylistic borrowings from Japa-nese theatre, Breuer and Maude Mitchell, who served as the dramaturg, describe their reasons for ignoring Kazan's interpretation:

> BREUER: Well, of course we were not going to reproduce a New Orleans street and apartment. This was not a remake of Kazan. This is not what I do, in the first place, and it isn't what I was brought to Paris to do....As for the elements from Japanese theatre, [Williams] once told the Japanese nov-elist Mishima that to understand the Japanese, you needed to be an inhabit-ant of the "decadent South," with "that mixture of brutality and elegance."
>
> MITCHELL: We hoped that the Japanese elements could suggest the cul-ture of honor, violence, and tradition in the idea of the "Old South." And we were not going to try to make a Southern French version of *Streetcar* like Cocteau did [in his 1949 stage production].[27]

Both Breuer and Mitchell frame the borrowings from Japanese theatre to better serve Williams's text without returning to Kazan's production as an authoritative model.[28] From the beginning of their process, their intentions were to distance the Comédie Française production from Ka-zan's American realism by creating a global relationship between Eastern elements and the Western text.

While the Japanese elements of the production emphasized honor, violence, and tradition, Twist's setting focused not on a real Japan but a Japan constructed almost entirely from a Western perspective.[29] When Blanche describes Stanley as an animal to Stella, a screen with a large tiger appeared, slowly opening to reveal Stanley overhearing their conversa-tion. Twist's integration of Japanese visuals also hinted at Japonisme, the Japanese influence on French impressionistic artists, such as Manet, De-gas, Seurat, and Monet, from exhibitions of Japanese prints in the nine-teenth century.[30] In sharp contrast to the normative memories connected to American interpretations of *Streetcar*, Twist's setting concretely em-phasized the exoticism of an imagined other, mirroring the oppressed identity of the characters—most notably, but not limited to, Blanche's victimization, Grey's homosexuality, and Stanley's struggles with class and masculinity.

Breuer's intentional staging of *Streetcar* against cultural memories as-sociated with Kazan's production resulted in a pronounced delocaliza-tion of the setting. This strategy of delocalization, furthered by Twist's use of screens, functioned similarly to Foucault's counter-memory. More-over, the delocalization of the setting allowed the relationship among the

American characters, French actors, and Eastern images to become part of the performance. By dismembering Williams's text from normative memories associated with American realism, Breuer created a global conversation about the relationship between Western and Eastern cultures, one that implied oppressed identities through the use of Japanese visuals.

Breuer used a similar process of delocalization in his approach to actor coaching, also in opposition to Kazan's realism. Kazan built his production around the differences in acting styles between the iconic performances of Jessica Tandy and Marlon Brando, which "helped create the contrast between the cultured woman from Belle Reve and the New Orleans 'Quarter' redneck."[31] Jessica Tandy's elocutionary style was modeled from British acting traditions, unlike Marlon Brando's more explosive Method acting style that he learned under Kazan's guidance at The Actor's Studio. In an interview, Kazan remembers the stark difference between the two acting styles: "[The Group Theatre] was the opposite to the then British tradition. The then British tradition was an imitation of behavior. That is, a person would study the external manifestations of a certain experience or emotion and imitate them. The Group actors would induce the actual emotion within themselves and then judge or try to control what came out."[32] When scholars document *Streetcar* as the triumph of Brando's Method performance over the weakness of Tandy's more presentational performance, they rely on mis-remembering the exploratory nature of these conflicting styles.[33]

In the Comédie Française production, Breuer guided the French actors away from both their classical training and any assumptions that *Streetcar* must be performed as American realism using Method Acting. Because Breuer faced a language barrier with the French actors, he used a stage manager and assistant director to translate his suggestions to the actors. This is not the first time Breuer has staged a play with non-English-speaking actors, having worked through translators with "Russian, Portuguese, German, Korean and Chinese actors."[34] In an interview, Breuer notes differences between French and American actors: "The biggest difference between French-trained actors and American ones is that the French approach is formal, intellectual from the 'outside,' rather than Stanislavskian….Their approach is through language and of course they are very highly trained in this."[35]

In order to free his actors from French conventions, Breuer worked with them using improvisation.[36] As director, Breuer added a sense of collaboration to the production, an element with which the French actors were not accustomed.[37] Throughout the process, Breuer continually relied on the input of the French actors and technicians, something "virtually unheard in France."[38] This process enabled a conversation between Breuer's avant-garde American directing style and the style of the French performers at the Comédie Française.

Breuer chose to distance his production from American realism based on his appreciation of surrealism and expressionism—not in opposition to reality—but as states of equal importance. For example, instead of having the characters sit around the poker table, Breuer staged the actors facing the audience. With screens representative of playing cards behind them, the actors depicted the card game expressionistically, using nonverbal sounds as they mimed playing nonexistent cards around a nonexistent table. In this scene Breuer also added comic touches such as Mitch stepping through a chair, Stanley getting his finger caught in a bottle, and Pablo rolling joints. Interpreting the scene in opposition to Kazan's realism also highlighted Williams's use of poker terms in the text as metaphors for conflict.[39] Breuer's staging of the poker scene did not focus on a realistic construction of place. As a counter-memory, Breuer's nonrealistic poker scene distanced his delocalized staging from Kazan's more localized, realistic version.

Breuer also conceived another radical departure for the most iconic moment crystallized in cultural memory by the film—Stanley standing at the bottom of a circular staircase yelling "Stella!" The memory of Brando's performance has become so popular that an annual Stella-screaming contest takes place in New Orleans with the prize going to the participant who can best imitate the intensity of Brando's performance.[40] To distance the visuals of this scene from any memories associated with the original, Breuer chose to place Stella floating on a wire over the stage in a billowing yellow dress. As she hovered over Stanley, who was kneeling on the ground—his nether-regions barely covered by a skimpy towel—Stella took Stanley in her arms. In a pose reminiscent of a Pieta, the pair then flew up into the catwalks for their sexual reconciliation.[41] Mitchell suggests Breuer's new staging of this moment points to a more powerful Stella, in opposition to Kazan's reading of Stella as Stanley's "narcotized slave."[42] By disregarding the American interpretation, clouded by naturalism, Breuer's production dismembered this culturally inscribed moment of the text. In essence, Breuer diffused the normative American memory associated with the localization of realistic New Orleans, using a more abstract physical embodiment that integrated the dramatic forms of several different cultures.

Another key disruption in Breuer's production was Eric Ruf's portrayal of Stanley. In the search for a more androgynous model for contemporary masculinity, Breuer chose to pattern his Stanley after Heath Ledger's performance of the Joker in Christopher Nolan's film *The Dark Knight*.[43]

In Breuer's production, before the rape of Blanche, Stanley entered in a green wig stolen from a Mardi Gras parade, donned purple pajamas, and covered his face in shaving cream. Although Breuer cites Ledger's sexual androgyny as the inspiration for this counter-memory, he admits that French audiences did not understand the reference, instead connecting this moment to Japanese Noh masks. This embodied counter-memory reveals the complexity of the global relationship in which American director and French audiences dismember the cultural references in this moment differently. Nevertheless, Ruf's more psychopathic Stanley upset the normative reading of Stanley's (Brando's) sanity in opposition to Blanche's (Tandy's) descent into madness. Amid the Eastern images and Japanese dramatic forms, the French actors did not rely on creating naturalistic characters, inhabiting a real, localized setting. I consider these disconnections from realism as global, because they cannot be read without a consideration of the relationships among the cultures involved.

Moreover, Breuer's reading utilized counter-memories that evoke nonnormative gender commentary, in direct contradiction to hegemonic cultural memories that suggest stable gender roles in *Streetcar*. In addition to Ruf's more androgynous Stanley, Breuer explored a more overtly sexual relationship between Stella and Blanche by having the sisters touch each other sensually.[44] After the iconic "Stella" screaming scene, Breuer interrupted the action with a drag performance by a Tunisian rock 'n' roll musician named Red One, who performed a New Orleans-inspired song called "Sticky Wicket" written by John Margolis. Breuer states that this disruption was intended to indicate "our Stanley's 'Rough Trade' qualities, which the original Stanley, of course, does not suggest."[45] Breuer's leather-clad Mitch, played by Gregory Gadebois, drove a motorcycle, representing the antithesis of Kazan's "he-man Mama's boy" as played by Karl Malden.[46] Breuer's interpretation of the characters relied predominantly on unconventional approaches to gender, achieved largely by exploring the ambiguity of sexual subcultures. When asked how audiences interpreted the contemporary commentary about gender, Breuer has asserted that, traditionally, gay audiences root for Blanche while straight audiences root for Stanley.[47] In considering these characters, Breuer dismembered his actors' performances from the iconic, comparatively more stable gender roles remembered in Kazan's film.

This dismembered exploration of character and gender stemmed from the global relationships explored in the rehearsal room. By calling into question the conventional gender roles of Kazan's *Streetcar*, Breuer guided his actors to nonnormative reconsiderations of Williams's characters. In a similar way to the integration of Eastern dramatic forms into the setting, these counter-memories made Breuer's *Streetcar* a more global interpretation—revealing perceptions of the American source material and the French actors and audiences, which were at odds with Kazan's more heteronormative, localized interpretation of the characters. When Hollywood got its hands on the script, it heavily censored the gay identity of Blanche's dead husband and changed the ending. In addition to deleting any references to homosexuality, the censor Joseph Breen insisted that Stanley be punished for assaulting Blanche.[48] By disconnecting from Kazan's Hollywood-ized production, Breuer delocalized the performances of his actors from both the conventions of American realistic acting and their training at the Comédie Française. Breuer's reading was filtered through French perceptions of imagined Japanese forms, creating a style for which the goal was not authenticity to any stabilized tradition, realistic or otherwise. Instead, Breuer's production relied on cultural exchange, exploring the global relationship between the American source, Japanese dramatic forms, and French theatrical practitioners.

Navigating hegemonic ideologies inscribed within the setting and acting style(s) of Kazan's production, Breuer also traversed resistance that French critics hold toward Williams as an American playwright. The French premiere of Cocteau's *Streetcar* in 1949 resulted in a largely negative reaction from French critics.[49] A similar reaction occurred with the French premiere of *Cat on a Hot Tin Roof*, directed by English auteur Peter Brook.[50] Critics of these earlier productions were quick to label the inherent sexuality of Williams's texts as depraved. French critics, during the 1940s and 1950s, fixated upon the perceived degeneracy of the characters, without referencing their struggles with morality.

In contrast, Breuer's production generated a more global conversation, demonstrating changing attitudes toward American theatre, homosexuality, and gender fluidity in France over the past sixty years.[51] At the end of a piece for the *New York Times*, Doreen Carvajal reduced the mixed reception by French critics to the following: "*Le Monde*'s review ran under the headline 'A *Streetcar* Stopped at the Boredom Station.' *Le Figaro*'s critic called the production 'powerful, profound, grand and unique.' The reviewer for *Les Echos* was more measured, observing that no one could have dreamed that one day Tennessee Williams would crash the house of Molière."[52]

The mixed response from critics demonstrates this shift to a more global conversation in comparison to the negative American stereotypes remembered from the French premieres. Consequently, Breuer's production used counter-memories to create new associations that replaced the earlier reduction of Williams to a stereotyped American, degenerate identity.

As theatre historians document Breuer's production, the importance of counter-memories and dismemberment becomes more apparent. Marvin

Carlson, in responding to a variety of French productions during that season, crafts a laudatory response to Breuer's innovations, describing Breuer's process as follows: "Many of the most famous moments of this familiar text are given startling and memorable, totally new configurations."[53] Along these lines, I would argue that dismembering—the act of reading Breuer's production as counter-memories—allows these totally new configurations to escape reinscription to the normative, localized, American memories surrounding Kazan's production. Aware of the importance of circumventing Kazan's shadow, Carlson specifically references Breuer's use of Japanese tropes. Rather than feed into the stereotypes of American drama that connect *Streetcar* with realism, Carlson demonstrates the need for practitioners and scholars to be open to new meanings that do not reinscribe traditional theatrical conventions and hegemonic meanings.[54]

In a similar fashion, David Savran, in "Tennessee Williams in France and Germany," highlights the elements of Japanese theatre as dismemberment: "Breuer's use of Japanese theatre has proven the most controversial feature of his *Streetcar*. Their application makes it clear that the play is not a naturalistic tragedy but a metatheatrical dream play about the staging of fantasy whose texture is repeatedly shattered by the force of memory and desire."[55] By noting what the delocalized features within Breuer's production add, Savran dismembers *Streetcar* from associations with naturalistic tragedy.[56] Although a metatheatrical dream play may seem at odds with Kazan's reading, Savran is quick to reconnect the visual elements from Breuer's production back to the remembered original: "Using the screens' capacity both to evoke movie screens and to cut the action in an almost cinematic way, Breuer pays homage to cinema and to Kazan without in any way reproducing Kazan's style."[57] When Savran reinscribes Breuer's choices as homage to Kazan, this inscription of the hegemonic memory could give authoritative power to the original at the expense of Breuer's rejection of *Streetcar* as institutionalized realism. However, both Carlson and Savran imply the need for scholars to frame Breuer's unconventional, idiosyncratic, and cosmopolitan production by pointing back to Kazan's realistic production as conventional because it is localized; the normative memories promote a reading of Kazan's setting and characters as realistic.

For the exploratory purposes of this analysis, I envision these four terms—counter-memories, dismember, global, and delocalization—as fluid and interconnected. However, through this exploration, the following pattern emerged. On the one hand, dismemberment and counter-memory relate entirely to the style of analysis I employed. Dismemberment is a reading style, a framework under which to collect disruptions to memory that are necessary to reconsider Breuer's production of *Streetcar* beyond assumptions made by normative critical inscription. Counter-memories are what is being read, embodied moments from the productions that concretely reveal the appropriateness of dismemberment as an alternate form of analysis. On the other hand, the terms global and delocalization are the results of this method for this particular project. I used dismemberment to consider the global relationships among the cultures involved without the reinscription of false memories surrounding Kazan's *Streetcar*. From the global relationships I examined, Breuer's strategy of delocalization (my term, not his) enabled a balance between the configuration of the different cultures and nonnormative elements of the production.

Using dismemberment as a method to enable a more global appreciation of Breuer's *Streetcar* is important for several reasons. First, production histories should question critical inscription rather than rely on this evidence, so heavily manipulated by normative consensus. Second, when considering a foreign production of a canonized American play, the historian can move beyond a simple compare/contrast between the authority of the American original and the "reinterpretation," as that style devalues the foreign contributions.[58] Finally, nonnormative productions of Tennessee Williams will only become more acceptable if critics and audiences begin to question *Streetcar*, and other similarly canonized works, as definitive examples of institutionalized American realism. Without cultivating this kind of awareness, which I identify collectively as dismemberment, international productions of American plays will continue to be read as misreadings of a normative original, which, in this case, never existed.

Notes

1. Matthew Biberman, "Tennessee Williams: The American Shakespeare," *Huffington Post*, March 26, 2011, http://www.huffingtonpost.com/matthew-biberman/tennessee-williams-the-am_b_838552.html, accessed November 29, 2015.

2. "The mockingly dismissive reviews of Ivo van Hove's fascinating, if flawed, production of *A Streetcar Named Desire* last fall at the New York Theatre Workshop provided further evidence, as though any more were needed, of their intractable conservatism. Faced with a nontraditional staging of Tennessee Williams's chestnut, they fell almost uniformly into battle formation." Charles McNulty, "Commuting beyond the Stereotypes: The Dangerous Trek of Ivo van Hove's *A Streetcar Named Desire*," *Theater* 30, no. 2 (Summer 2000): 155, http:/muse.jhu.edu/article/34096, accessed April 30, 2016.

3. Michel Foucault, Donald F. Bouchard, and Sherry Simon, *Language,*

Counter-memory, Practice: Selected Essays and Interviews (Ithaca, N.Y.: Cornell University Press, 1977), 155.

4. Ibid., 160.

5. Quoted in Phillip Kolin, *Williams: A Streetcar Named Desire* (Cambridge: Cambridge University Press, 2000), 24.

6. In a letter from Williams to Elia Kazan, dated April 19, 1947, he states: "It is a tragedy with the classic aim of producing a catharsis of pity and terror, and in order to do that Blanch must finally have the understanding and compassion of the audience. This without creating a black-dyed villain in Stanley." Tennessee Williams, Albert J. Devlin, and Nancy Tischler, *The Selected Letters of Tennessee Williams: Volume 2, 1945–1957* (New York: New Directions, 2004), 95–97.

7. Nancy Tischler, *Student Companion to Tennessee Williams* (Westport, Conn.: Greenwood Press, 2000), 53.

8. Kathleen Margaret Lant, "A Streetcar Named Misogyny," in *Violence in Drama*, ed. James Redmond (Cambridge: Cambridge University Press, 1991), 225–38.

9. "Instead, I think the problem is a false opposition between the local and the global. Both are implicated in globalization. The 'other' of globalization is not the local but cosmopolitanism." For a more detailed comparison between globalization in opposition to localization, see Dan Rebellato, *Theater & Globalization* (New York: Palgrave Macmillan, 2009), 59.

10. Dale Southerton, *Encyclopedia of Consumer Culture* (Thousand Oaks, Calif.: Sage Publications, 2011), 431.

11. Ibid.

12. Susan Bennett and Christie Carson, *Shakespeare beyond English: A Global Experiment* (Cambridge: Cambridge University Press, 2013); Laurence Senelick, *The Chekhov Theatre: A Century of the Plays in Performance* (Cambridge: Cambridge University Press, 1997).

13. Artistic Director Muriel Mayette admits she chose Breuer because she wanted "to shake up the Comédie Française." Lee Breuer, Maude Mitchell, and Joan Templeton, "The First American Play at the Comédie Française: Lee Breuer Directs Tennessee Williams," *PAJ: A Journal of Performance and Art* 35, no. 1 (January 2013): 81–82.

14. "What we found in *Colonus* was that we had a wonderful new key to classical narrative—a didactic or oratorical device—by using the preaching rhythm inherent in the Baptist and Pentecostal churches. The black church experience here is a wonderful new idea about tragic rhythms and, who knows, maybe closer to what the original Greek performances were like." Lee Breuer, interview with Gerald Rabkin, "Lee Breuer: On *The Gospel at Colonus*," *Performing Arts Journal* 8, no. 1 (1984): 49.

15. "Patriarchy is in reality three feet tall, but has a voice that will dominate six-foot women." Quoted in Gerald Rabkin, "Lee Breuer's Classic Comics," *Performing Arts Journal* 26, no. 2 (May 2004): 44.

16. Gabrielle Cody and Lee Breuer, "Lee Breuer on Interculturalism," *Performing Arts Journal* 11, no. 3 (1989): 62.

17. To define the difference between embodied and inscribed memories, I conflate the performative theories of Diana Taylor with the memory theories of Paul Connerton. In *The Archive and the Repertoire*, Taylor proposes the necessity of counterbalancing the dominance of textually inscribed archival memories with embodied evidence: Diana Taylor, *The Archive and the Repertoire* (Durham, N.C.: Duke University Press, 2003), 16. Paul Connerton identifies a similar balance between inscribed and incorporating practices—history favors textual evidence because it exists in a stable form: Paul Connerton, *How Societies Remember* (Cambridge: Cambridge University Press, 1989), 78–79. They both explore the supposed binary relationship between written and performed memories.

18. Breuer, Mitchell, and Templeton, "The First American Play at the Comédie Française: Lee Breuer Directs Tennessee Williams," 91.

19. For more on Williams's early theories about theatrical form see Richard E. Kramar, "The Sculptural Drama: Tennessee Williams's Plastic Theatre," *Tennessee Williams Annual Review* 5 (2002): 1, http://www.tennesseewilliamsstudies.org/journal/work.php?ID=45, accessed February 1, 2016.

20. Mary C. Henderson, *Mielziner: Master of Modern Stage Design* (New York: Back Stage Books, 2001), 13–26.

21. "The environment was established by using three levels of transparency.... The architectural detail is frankly distorted. No attempt is made to suggest that walls and windows are real." Harry W. Smith documents Mielziner's designs for the sets and lights of *Glass Menagerie, Streetcar*, and *Summer and Smoke* in "Tennessee Williams and Jo Mielziner: The Memory Plays," *Theatre Survey* 23, no.2 (November 1983): 227.

22. Sam Staggs collects anecdotes of the journey of *Streetcar* from Broadway to Hollywood, noting differences between historical narratives and interviews both before and after the Hollywood censorship in Sam Staggs, *When Blanche Met Brando: The Scandalous Story of "A Streetcar Named Desire"* (New York: St. Martin's Press, 2005).

23. Breuer and Twist discuss the screens at length during the interview hosted at the Philoctetes Center: Enoch Brater, Lee Breuer, Roger Copeland, Joe Jeffreys, Maude Mitchell, and Basil Twist, "Realism and Expressionism in the Work of Tennessee Williams," Philoctetes Center, uploaded on April 6, 2011, https://www.youtube.com/watch?v+EkWX6ACGA9k, accessed September 15, 2015.

24. Directed by Lee Breuer with animated design and puppetry by Basil Twist, *Red Beads* premiered in September 2005 at New York University. Twist's designs are described on the Mabou Mines website as follows: "Using only wind, Basil Twist transforms swaths of fabric into luminous, quivering, ephemeral sets and puppets—along the way challenging our perception of space and proportion." "*Red Beads*," *Mabou Mines*, http://www.maboumines.org/production/red-beads/, accessed September 11, 2016.

25. Ibid. Breuer also states during the roundtable that his collaboration with Twist was unconventional. Although the Comédie Française requires a single

director and a single set designer, Breuer asserts that they designed and directed in tandem.

26. According to Staggs, Ballard costumed the production in opposition to Williams's descriptions: "Ballard claimed that one reason the London production didn't do better was that Olivier had slavishly followed Tennessee's costume descriptions rather than her own revisions of them for Broadway." Staggs, *When Blanche Met Brando*, 189.

27. Breuer, Mitchell, and Templeton, "The First American Play at the Comédie Française," 88–89.

28. This was in contrast to the Japanese premiere, which emphasized Occidentalist American identity, as staged by the Bungakuza Dramatic company in 1953, covered in Kolin, *Williams: A Streetcar Named Desire*, 76–82.

29. Breuer and Twist imagine Japan in a similar fashion to how Edward Said constructs his theories of Orientalism: "One ought never to assume that the structure of Orientalism is nothing more than a structure of lies or myths which, were the truth about them to be told, would simply blow away." Edward Said, *Orientalism* (New York: Pantheon, 1978), 6.

30. "An important reason for the assimilation of Oriental ideas by French artists is that many of the Japanese elements they encountered corresponded with effects they had noticed and admired in their own environment." Gabriel P. Weisberg, *Japonisme: Japanese Influence on French Art, 1854–1910* (Cleveland: Cleveland Museum of Art, 1975), 116.

31. Elia Kazan, *Elia Kazan: A Life* (New York: Alfred A. Knopf, 1988), 344.

32. Michel Ciment, *Kazan on Kazan* (New York: Viking, 1974), 34.

33. "Although the Studio did not set out deliberately to abolish the older, elocutionary acting brought over from England—Tandy's style, also the style of Helen Hayes, Katharine Cornell, Lunt and Fontanne, the Barrymores, and other legends—it did so, and fast." Staggs, *When Brando Met Blanche*, 87. John Lahr summarizes this as follows: "[Brando's] characterization of Stanley was so strong that it threatened to overpower Tandy and to throw the play off kilter." This generalization is drawn from Brando's and Kazan's memories. John Lahr, *Tennessee Williams: Mad Pilgrimage of the Flesh* (New York: W. W. Norton, 2014), 142.

34. Breuer, Mitchell, and Templeton, "The First American Play at the Comédie Française," 85.

35. Ibid.

36. "Another key thing: we had to teach the actors to improvise. They were used to planning everything in advance, to a 'T,' in rehearsals, and then executing it." Ibid., 88. "'In France, for reasons of time and production, we have a tendency to follow the road, and Lee works on the journey and the passage,' said Mr. Ruf [who played Stanley]....'We are generally very precise about movement and advancement. With him, we are improvising.'" Doreen Carvajal, "French *Streetcar* in Paris, Stanley but No T-Shirt" *New York Times*, February 22, 2011, http://www.nytimes.com/2011/02/15/arts/15comedie.html?_r=0, accessed February 23, 2015.

37. This sense of exploration indicates what Fischer calls Breuer's postmodern

style, more exploratory than didactic: "As the director of the three Beckett pieces that brought Mabou Mines to Papp's attention, Breuer was completing, in a sense, his love affair with absurdism and existentialism. Henceforth, he would live and write in a postabsurdist, postmodern vein." Iris Smith Fischer, *Mabou Mines: Making Avant-garde Theater in the 1970s* (Ann Arbor: University of Michigan Press, 2011), 98.

38. Breuer and Mitchell recount specific events from the production, which include suggestions from Françoise Gillard about Stella's character, Eric Ruf's contrast from the traditional way French actors work, and the chief sound man, who said Breuer was the first director who ever asked his opinion. Breuer, Mitchell, and Templeton, "The First American Play at the Comédie Française," 86.

39. An earlier title of the scene was "The Poker Night," evident in the text with references such as "Lay your cards on the table" and "The game is seven card stud." In translating these metaphors to a French context, Breuer decided on "Joker's Wild" as the final poker reference. Tennessee Williams, *A Streetcar Named Desire*, in *Plays 1937–1955* (New York: Library of America, 2000), 488, 564.

40. Staggs frames the annual contest as evidence of the cultural popularity of the film. Staggs, *When Blanche Met Brando*, 10–11.

41. Unless otherwise noted, comments from Breuer, Twist, and Mitchell come from the Philoctetes Center Roundtable: Brater, Breuer, Copeland, Jeffreys, Mitchell, and Twist, "Realism and Expressionism in the Work of Tennessee Williams."

42. Kim Hunter's performance, captured in the film, documents Kazan's interpretation of Stella's sexual dependency on Stanley. In Kazan's directing notes, he gives each character a spine that, I assert, imposes a straight, hegemonic, inscribed interpretation of Williams's text; the sections on Stella and Mitch are particularly revealing. Elia Kazan, "Notebook for *A Streetcar Named Desire*," in *Directors on Directing*, ed. Toby Cole and Helen Krich Chinoy (Indianapolis: Bobbs-Merrill, 1963), 364–79.

43. Whether or not Ledger's performance could be considered more "androgynous" than Brando's Stanley is debatable, but "androgynous" is the word that Breuer uses to describe his reasons for choosing Ledger's Joker as inspiration. Brater, Breuer, Copeland, Jeffreys, Mitchell, and Twist, "Realism and Expressionism in the Work of Tennessee Williams," Philoctetes Center Roundtable.

44. "With their petting and nuzzling, the sisters form a nearly incestuous pair, so that Blanche's demise sets off a dramatic depression in postpartum Stella." Molly Grogan, "A *Streetcar* to Paris via New York," *Paris Voice*, February 8, 2011, http://maboumines.org/press/paris-voice-streetcar-paris-new-york, accessed August 10, 2016.

45. Breuer, Mitchell, and Templeton, "The First American Play at the Comédie Française," 90.

46. "Notebook for *A Streetcar Named Desire*," in Cole and Chinoy, *Directors on Directing*, 364–79.

47. Brater, Breuer, Copeland, Jeffreys, Mitchell, and Twist, "Realism and Expressionism in the Work of Tennessee Williams," Philoctetes Center Roundtable.

48. Kazan and Williams were aware of some of the censorship during the film's

production, but the Legion of Decency also made cuts that neither of them approved. Lahr, *Tennessee Williams: Mad Pilgrimage of the Flesh*, 229–32; Staggs, *When Brando Met Blanche*, 241–57.

49. Reviews from the French premiere of *Streetcar* quoted in Kolin include remarks such as "filled with undressing, morbid events, fights, card games, enough alcohol to drown in, obscenities, and murders" and "a fantasy seeking play that does not go above the waistline with huge naked monkeys, climbing down trees to dance under the neon signs of advertisements." Kolin, *Williams: A Streetcar Named Desire*, 71–72.

50. Reviews from Brook's production were just as stigmatized against American depravity, calling *Cat* "melodramatic filth," "crude heavy drama of sexuality," and "confused tragedy, gross and heated, and very noisy." Richard Helfer and Glenn Loney, *Peter Brook: Oxford to Orghast* (Amsterdam: Harwood Academic Publishers, 1998), 85.

51. In *The Elastic Closet*, Scott Gunther examines how attitudes have changed regarding gay identity since the 1942 law that separated the age of consent. In his conclusion, written in 2009, Gunther speculates "on the effects of recent arrival of American queer theory in France." Scott Gunther, *The Elastic Closet: A History of Homosexuality in France, 1942–present* (London: Palgrave Macmillan, 2009), 121.

52. Carvajal, "French *Streetcar* in Paris, Stanley but No T-Shirt."

53. Marvin Carlson, "April in Paris," *Western European Stages* 23, no. 3 (Fall 2011): 107.

54. In *The Haunted Stage*, Marvin Carlson describes all theatre as a memory machine, where performances, sometimes unconsciously, reference previous models in a chain of iteration, which has no specific origin, a process he calls ghosting: "Theater, as a simulacrum of the cultural and historical process itself, seeking to depict the full range of human actions within their physical context, has always provided society with the most tangible records of its attempts to understand its own operations. It is the repository of cultural memory, but, like the memory of each individual, it is also subject to continual adjustment and modification as the memory is recalled in new circumstances and contexts." Marvin Carlson, *The Haunted Stage: The Theatre as Memory Machine* (Ann Arbor: University of Michigan, 2001), 2.

55. David Savran, "Tennessee Williams in France and Germany," in *Tennessee Williams and Europe: Intercultural Encounters, Transatlantic Exchanges*, ed. John S. Bak (Amsterdam: Rodopi, 2014), 275.

56. As early as the premiere, critics were quick to label *Streetcar* as a tragedy. "It is almost unbearably tragic," wrote Brooks Atkinson in "Mr. Williams' Report on Life in New Orleans," *New York Times*, December 14, 1947.

57. Ibid.

58. Enoch Brater edited a collection about the global reception of Arthur Miller: "It is perhaps one of the great oddities of Miller's long career as an important American writer—one, moreover, with such vivid nativist credentials— that some of the strongest responses to his plays have consistently come from abroad." Enoch Brater, *Arthur Miller's Global Theater* (Ann Arbor: University of Michigan Press, 2007), 6.

Transformative Cross-Cultural Dialogue in Prague

Americans Creating Czech History Plays

Karen Berman

Through a series of study abroad journeys, students at Georgia College under my direction as the chair of the Department of Theatre and Dance have presented original plays that address, from an American standpoint, Czech heroes who fought the Communist and Nazi regimes. The plays, co-written by me and my husband, Paul Accettura, and directed by me, have fostered cross-cultural dialogue between Czech audiences and American actors as we brought both well-known and little-known personages of the Czech Republic to life for the Czech people. Performances took place in Prague theatres and museums and in the Eastern European Regions International Theatre Festival in Hradac Kralove during the summers of 2010, 2012, and 2014. Indirectly describing our experiences with Czech theatres, Dan Rebellato in his book *Theatre & Globalization* states: "The ever-greater interconnectedness of theatre cultures is visible in the post-war phenomenon of the international festival."[1] Although not all Georgia College performances in the Czech Republic have occurred during international festivals, the pursuit of cross-cultural dialogue seems to be a shared goal.

Utilizing global theatre techniques of Czech, Polish, and American theatre, the Georgia College summer productions have energized physical theatre practices for the American actors involved, and framed historical movements of the Czech Republic for Czech audiences from an outsiders' perspective. Georgia College students who participated in the study abroad encounters were immersed in Grotowski's ideographs and the political theatre of playwright Vaclav Havel. Havel, who led a peaceful revolution against Communism in then Czechoslovakia, is a principal example of an artist who successfully promoted social change, influencing many countries, most particularly his own. Grotowski's ideographs—images embodied by the actors—along with dance elements used to further the visual storytelling allowed key parts of the three plays to be told without words to audience members who were not fully fluent in English. The ideographs were also very effective in dramatizing the lives, thoughts, and events impacting important figures from Czech history due to their ability to help the actors embody emotional and political conflict.

The experience of performing Czech stories in the Czech Republic gave students from the United States global awareness into the characters and histories of Central European people through theatre. By conducting dramaturgical research into the political and cultural situations of the time periods and locations covered by the plays, students perceived how global events impacted the Czech characters they were depicting. Additionally, their interactions with Czech people during the rehearsal and performance processes, as well as interactions with key sites in the Czech Republic relevant to the arc of their character's journeys, provided opportunities for transformative cross-cultural dialogue and learning. The Georgia College students were able to discuss US and European culture, politics, and history with a variety of theatre artists present at the festival from countries throughout Europe. This frequently provided the students with a better picture of how the United States, its politics, and its culture are understood from the perspective of European theatre artists. Perhaps most importantly, these discussions often provided the students with surprising critiques of US political culture. The following account attempts to unpack our experiences and illuminate at least one approach to fostering transformative cross-cultural dialogue through theatre.

Perhaps not surprisingly, the logistical challenges of presenting new plays in another country, in English, based on important historical characters from that country, performed by American actors, initially seemed daunting. Through Georgia College's vice president of international education, Dr. Dwight Call, we were able to find a host in the Czech Republic. Dr. Stanislav Bohadlo, a music professor at the University of Hradac Králové who is fluent in English and well connected within the theatre and music communities there, served as host and interpreter. He was able to assist us in acquiring a space in which to perform during each of our visits at the international theatre festival in Hradac Králové, and we timed our visits to coincide with the festival. Dr. Bohadlo was also able to arrange rehearsal space at his university and at his small theatre building (a converted barn) in the charming baroque-era town of Kuks, near Hradac Králové. As an added bonus, two of Dr. Bohadlo's young adult children are actors affiliated with Geisslers Hofcomoedianten, a theatre company in Prague that also performed as part of the international festival. They generously gave the student actors insights into the Czech theatre community.

Preparation for each play involved extensive dramaturgical research, conducted by my co-author and me, on the heroes and history of Czechoslovakia and the Czech Republic that were dramatized in each of the plays. Specific Czech heroes, such as Havel, were selected because of their importance to Czech history or their relevance to the general character of the Czech people. The research, dramaturgy, and basic writing of each of the plays took place over several months before the students began rehearsals. Eventually, through a collaborative process, students' perspectives were transformed as they conducted their own research in preparation for performing in the plays. By investigating the people and history of the country they were to perform in, students developed their own characterizations of uniquely Czech characters; in addition, the rehearsal process for each play immersed the students in the traumatic history of Czechoslovakia and the Czech Republic. The real-life characters they portrayed lived through the Nazi occupation, the Holocaust, brief periods of a free Czechoslovakia, the Communist era, the reforms of the 1968 Prague Spring and its repression by Soviet and Eastern bloc troops and tanks, and the Velvet Revolution that overthrew the Communist regime. As a result of participating in these rehearsal processes, the students' learning was greatly enhanced, as they absorbed history through the eyes of the characters they were portraying. Student learning was especially impacted by specific site visits within the Czech Republic, including the Balustrade Theatre in Prague, where many of Havel's most famous plays were first produced, and the fascinating Kafka Museum in Prague, which has a confining design intended to take the visitor into the mind of Franz Kafka. Not surprisingly, the Terezín concentration camp proved to be the most impactful site visited. More than just historical sites, these locations were significant to the journeys of the characters the students portrayed and immersed the students into Czech and European history and culture.

For the purposes of this essay, I have chosen to focus on the first of our plays produced in the Czech Republic, *The Women of Havel and Kafka*. The play focuses largely on Havel, a playwright who became president of free Czechoslovakia following the Velvet Revolution. Working on the play helped the students to understand Havel's influence on the country in which they studied and performed, as well as the impact of theatre as a potential agent of social change. The significance of Havel's work to the Czech people and its effect on broader cultural change was a key part of the learning experience in the rehearsal processes for all three of the plays we wrote and produced in the Czech Republic. Through dramaturgical research, the students learned that Havel's works were revolutionary to the Czech Republic because they solidified and lent key support to a developing underground movement of anti-Communist sentiment. The students also realized that Havel's theatrical works satirized Communist bureaucracy, a quality that most people can relate to globally, since we tend to suffer from bureaucracy on a personal level. Likewise, in learning about Havel's reluctance to become a politician, with all the troubles and compromises associated, students also discovered his surprising decision to stop writing plays. All of these experiences and findings contributed to the students' layered conception of Havel and Czech culture.

In order to provide the students with an understanding of Czech history and the country's rich and complex artistic culture, a visit to Terezín was particularly important. From 1942 to 1945 Terezín imprisoned all Bohemian and Moravian Jews and was a "hotbed of cultural activity," including "cabaret evenings…and…plays for adults."[2] The students' visit to the camp helped them to imagine what many European artists suffered through during the Nazi occupation as Jewish, homosexual, and politically leftist artists were imprisoned and often died there simply because of their religion, sexual orientation, and political views. Not surprisingly, the troubling nature of this visit was apparent in the students' demeanors, as it expanded their understanding of the Czech characters that lived through this fraught time in history. Through this absorption of Czech culture, the students were able to develop a complex portrait of the country and its character as they prepared to embody real-life people from recent Czech history in the play. As Havel wrote, "Theatre is an art form so social that, more than any other art form, it depends on having a public existence, and that means it is at the mercy of cultural conditions."[3] Likewise, the students were able to give our work a public existence facilitating the cross-cultural dialogue that developed in the process. What is more, the positive reactions of the Czech audiences were a gratifying aspect of the experience for all of us in light of Havel's prominence as a public figure.

In order to provide greater context for the significance of Havel's work and, therefore, our production, it is important to consider aspects of Havel's life and influence. Havel's plays were an essential part of the economic, cultural, and political evolution of the Czech people during and immediately after the Communist era. As Jarka Burian puts it, Havel lived through "the liberation from the swastika followed by subjugation to the hammer and sickle."[4] The fact that Havel remained a resident of Czechoslovakia through both the Nazi occupation and the entire Communist era makes him relatively unusual among internationally known Communist era dissident artists, many of whom went into exile. Despite this oppressive past, in which Communist regimes repressed speech and theatre that was not sympathetic to Communist ideology, Havel remained an influence throughout the Communist era in Czechoslovakia. Because performances of his plays were common in Western countries and banned in Communist Czechoslovakia, the scripts were passed around secretly in Czechoslovakia, thereby retaining their influence.[5] Given this repressive history, in contrast I appreciated the freedom to write and direct *The Women of Havel and Kafka* in the Czech Republic, an opportunity that is indicative of the current cultural freedom there that Havel helped to create.

Havel's work is part of a long tradition of Czech theatre created through adversity. As the Terezín theatre tradition demonstrates, the strength of Czech theatre continued even during the Holocaust. After World War II and prior to the full seizure of power by the Communists in Czechoslovakia in February 1948, many Czech theatres were operated for private profit, and all of them were placed under state control in 1948 when the Communists seized power there.[6] Czech theatre was heavily subsidized by the state, and Prague had twenty thriving professional theatres in the late 1960s, each subsidized at about 70 percent of their total expenses.[7] The uniqueness of the Czech experience under Communism is exemplified by the cultural and political openness of the Prague Spring of 1968, which was followed by its subsequent suppression. The invasion of Czechoslovakia by the Soviet Union and its Warsaw Pact allies in August 1968 ended the liberal reforms. Havel and the Balustrade Theatre had been in the forefront of these reforms of the Communist system, and their performances energized the public against the excesses of autocratic political and economic systems.

The famous Balustrade Theatre of Czechoslovakia (now the Czech Republic) produced Havel's influential plays in the 1960s. Havel began as a stagehand there and became their dramaturg just before his play *The Garden Party* was produced.[8] When I visited the still-thriving theatre in June 2009 I was surprised at its size, with about 200 seats in front of a very small stage that measured approximately eighteen by twenty-five feet. I was also shown the backstage, which revealed virtually no fly or offstage space as well as a tiny light booth. During future study abroad programs, I took student actors from all three plays to visit the Balustrade Theatre as a lesson in the power of theatre as an agent of social change. Students were shocked at the small size and intimacy of a space that was such a powerful part of effecting social change in Czechoslovakia. It was a revelation to us all that this unassuming, intimate space had such historic influence.

In keeping with the intimacy of Havel's original theatrical home, *The Women of Havel and Kafka* focuses on the familiarity shown through the language of gesture between Havel and his wife, Olga, also incorporating a similar language of gesture in depicting Kafka's influence on Havel. The play portrays a stunningly eventful life of artists, activists, and leaders thriving in a difficult period during which Havel suffered imprisonment several times. Both Kafka and Havel serve as representatives of a society that questioned its own culture and politics. As Marketa Goetz-Stankiewicz states, "Havel never permits us to formulate a comfortably assured answer; rather, like Kafka or Beckett, he opens a myriad of questions which seem to extend out of sight."[9] This self-questioning is characteristic of the Czech people even today. In *The Women of Havel and Kafka* the characters' suffering in the Communist economic and political system is key, as is their questioning of its power—both of which were portrayed through the language of gestures in our production.

The Women of Havel and Kafka was produced at the 2010 Theatre European Regions International Theatre Festival in Hradec Králové in the Czech Republic. Much of the text was inspired by Havel's plays and nonfiction works, as well as letters written by him from prison to Olga. A study of gender, *The Women of Havel and Kafka* highlights the roles of the women who inspired and aided Havel through their support during his imprisonments and the suppression of his works. More specifically, the play focuses on both of Havel's wives, Olga and Dagmar, and their influences on his work. The play also addresses Kafka's works and his critique of a bureaucratic, autocratic society as an important impact on Havel.

The Women of Havel and Kafka depicts both men as victims of a terrifyingly autocratic society, particularly in twentieth-century Czechoslovakia. Yet the reception for our performance of the play, including three curtain calls, reflects positive changes in freedom of expression in the Czech Republic. Such change is also evidenced in the openness of the people's positive responses to the appearance of the character of Olga, Havel's first wife. Once a dissident publicly hated by the Communist government, she is now openly revered there. Throughout Havel's political ordeal, Olga remained forceful and committed as he was "imprisoned or detained at least a half-dozen times for a total of some five years after 1969...and prevented from having any of his writings published or performed in his own country for over twenty years."[10]

Even though *The Women of Havel and Kafka* was performed in English, the Czech audience understood the play, in part, through our use of gesture. Grotowski's ideographs served to illuminate the storytelling for an audience not fully fluent in the English of the play's text. According to Thomas Richards, who worked extensively with Grotowski, physical actions are central to his work.[11] Famed Living Theatre director Peter Brook said it best in his preface to *Towards a Poor Theatre* in which he discussed

Grotowski's method: "The work is essentially nonverbal. To verbalise is to complicate and even to destroy exercises that are clear and simple when indicated by a gesture and executed by the mind and body as one."[12] As a director, such embodiment of expression was my goal in using the ideographs to stage cross-cultural plays using US student actors for an international audience. In keeping with Grotowski's practice, during our rehearsal process we relied "on improvisation or a scenario developed by performers and a director"[13] to create wordless sections of performance that expressed the journey of the characters through motivated physical actions inspired by research and character work. We incorporated the ideographs in improvised gestures of human emotions such as love, represented by creative physical hugs and caresses between Havel and Olga, and fear, indicated by Kafka's backward and off-balance movements as he wrestles with his troubled mind. In addition, these wordless sections of performance—representing the mind and body as one—included improvised dance and the creation of jail cells, airplanes, barbed-wire barricades, and tanks by the ensemble using only their bodies. As the students performed these nonverbal, ideographic sections, music from Czech composers of the twentieth century, sound effects, and nationalistic music were utilized to support movement and add impact. Our Czech and international audiences appreciated the use of gesture as part of our shared cross-cultural dialogue. Following performances, the students received feedback from members of the audience, who almost universally noted that the movements, gestures, and dance-like movements helped their understanding of the play.

Arguably, the use of ideographs in *The Women of Havel and Kafka* was effective for the Czech audience, in part because they were able to observe the unspoken bonds between the women in the play and between Havel and Kafka. Within the play, both of the men struggle with real and imagined demons in their given cultures, reaching out to women to sustain them through troubled times. For example, at the start of several scenes, the character of Kafka is shown physically spinning almost out of control as he grapples with internal demons and then is physically caught from falling by each of the women who support him as he leans on them, each in a different tableau. In Havel's case, Olga had been his strongest supporter and encouraged his life in the theatre against the wishes of his family, especially his mother. Within the play, Olga's gestures of warm support for Havel as he broods over the burdens of fighting authority and surviving prison include leaning on his shoulder and other physical expressions of comfort. In another sequence, Olga holds him and circles him seductively as he sits with his head down and his hand to his chin, similarly to Rodin's sculpture *The Thinker*. In *The Women of Havel and*

Kafka, these ideographic gestures showing Olga's empathy and support are emphasized as long-standing and essential aspects of Havel's ability to maintain his work through two decades of oppression under the political and economic system imposed after 1968. Sadly, the country's beloved Olga died while Havel was still in office, leaving the emotionally needy Havel without a strong woman to support him, and leading, in turn, to Havel's marriage to his second wife, Dagmar, a well-known Czech actress.

In *The Women of Havel and Kafka*, Dagmar's consumerism stands in strong contrast to Olga's calm restraint. Within the context of our play, Dagmar's portrayal included physical gestures of egotistical posturing, including arms crossed and a pouty face when she did not get her way, as well as a flirty twirl with one arm in the air in a charmingly irresistible seductive dance. In this way, the developing market economy and freedom of the post-Velvet Revolution with its consumerism and increasing selfishness were represented in the play by gestures of vanity enacted by Dagmar. Likewise, the warmth, comfort, and selflessness expressed in Olga's gestures in the play provided a mirror of women in Czechoslovakia during the economic and cultural repression of the post-1968 economy. In our depiction of post-1968 Czechoslovakia, Olga's gestures represented survival, while Dagmar's gestures displayed her consumer choices in post-1996 Czechoslovakia. These purposefully contrasting images within the play also served to showcase Havel's evolution from a dissident writer to a politician with a political staff, often troubled as he tried to lead his nation through economic and political difficulties and his wives tried to negotiate the very different expectations of their own respective roles. Olga was noted for her work "to empower the downtrodden" while Dagmar was at odds with Havel's presidential staff over her political and social demands, resulting in negative press coverage and Havel's personal concern with the dislike Dagmar seemed to generate among his political allies.[14]

Despite Havel's transformative work, as the heroine of *The Women of Havel and Kafka*, Olga is representative of the long-suffering Czech people. In the play it is Olga who embodies Havel's interests and beliefs in a free society that she fully shared with him. The many people who felt solidarity for those beliefs, but who were unable to publicly express their support due to the repressions of the Communist system, likely found comfort in Olga's strength while Havel was imprisoned. Olga's support for her husband as he fought economic and cultural repression was also her fight against male state power. While twenty years later Havel's dissident challenges to the economic system won out, there were two decades during which Communism persisted. The average citizen in Czechoslovakia was forced to accept economic and social repression in a situation where improvement was simply not feasible.

As *The Women of Havel and Kafka* portrays, Havel had no power within his own nation for those twenty years, except as an underground dissident celebrated in other countries. While his plays were performed in many parts of the world, he did not see them performed in his own country during that time. During our rehearsal process, learning and internalizing these details about Havel's life led the student actors to begin to understand the power and sacrifice involved in being an artist working to effect social change. In the play, they portrayed Havel's leadership as a visible and internationally known artist and dissident who was willing to submit peacefully to prison. His willingness to go to prison eventually took its toll on the viability of the economic and cultural system, slowly helping to foment political change. Havel's consistent artistic activism makes it especially intriguing that after the Velvet Revolution brought an entirely new economic system to Czechoslovakia, he stopped writing plays. While Havel was, of course, occupied with his newly acquired political responsibilities, it is still surprising that he simply ended his prior lifetime of work as a playwright. The fact that his plays were a reaction to an economic and political system that his writing had helped to end leads one to the conclusion that once that oppressive economic system ended, his need to write plays ended too. The language of gesture in *The Women of Havel and Kafka* indicates this, depicting Havel's physical movements turning inward after the initial euphoria of the Velvet Revolution that finally overthrew the Communist regime in 1989.

Utilizing Grotowski-style ideographs, *The Women of Havel and Kafka* revealed the sources of Havel's inspiration—the women in his life—as well as the influence of Kafka. In this initial play, and in two subsequent plays, *The Flights of Jan Weiner*[15] and *The Mystery of Mucha*,[16] the ideographs helped to establish, through nonverbal means, an ongoing cross-cultural dialogue lending complexity to the storylines. All three of these plays, their processes, and the visits to the Czech Republic provided students with opportunities to experience cross-cultural dialogue in ways that will have a lasting and transformative impact. The Georgia College students were impressed with the seriousness and the artistic creativity of the Czech theatrical community, seeing several productions during the festival and discussing theatre at length with the Czech people they met. Dramaturgical research on the Czech characters they portrayed, interactions with the Czech people, visits to historical sites, and lectures at the University of Hradac Králové helped to open the eyes of the students, expanding their worldview.

A particular example of student transformation is demonstrated by their growing self-awareness. Through their interactions with people of all ages in the Czech Republic, the students perceived that the Czech people did not appear happy. As longtime Georgia residents, the students were accustomed to southern hospitality and outward friendliness and smiles, which are common in public interactions in Georgia. Those easy smiles were not to be seen in the Czech Republic. What the students quickly realized is that the ready, friendly smiles and pleasantries that are so common in the southeastern United States were viewed as artificial by the Czech people. Through their experiences they came to understand that the Czech people had been under the subjugation of many other cultures and political systems with only brief times of self-rule. The Austro-Hungarian Empire, the Nazi occupation, and Communist rule have had a long-lasting impact on the people of the Czech Republic. The students' transformation came in their understanding of why the Czech people did not smile as people typically do in Georgia. It also began an important self-reflection by the Georgia College students about southern hospitality in the United States and whether it is, in fact, artificial—possibly masking US problems of racism and gun violence, issues that were noted by the Czech people when they asked the students about their home country. Accompanying this realization, the Georgia College students also learned that the Czech people knew as much, if not more, about current US events and politics than they did. It was also clear that the Czech people were fully aware of the power US politics had on their lives in a globalized world. As the students' research, rehearsal process, and subsequent performances in the Czech Republic show, experiencing cross-cultural dialogue on site is a transformative act. This kind of artistic cultural immersion deepens cross-cultural knowledge and understanding in immeasurable ways, facilitating that transformation.

Notes

1. Dan Rebellato, *Theatre & Globalization* (New York: Palgrave Macmillan, 2009), 8.

2. Jarka Burian, *Modern Czech Theatre: Reflector and Conscience of a Nation* (Iowa City: University of Iowa Press, 2000), 62–63.

3. Vaclav Havel, *Open Letters: Selected Writings 1965–1990* (New York: Vintage Books, 1992), 5–6.

4. Jarka Burian, *Leading Creators of Twentieth-Century Czech Theatre* (New York: Routledge, 2002), 204.

5. Carol Rocamora, *Acts of Courage: Vaclav Havel's Life in the Theater* (Hanover, N.H.: Smith and Kraus, 2004).

6. Ibid., 69.

7. Ibid., 139.

8. Burian, *Modern Czech Theatre*.

9. Marketa Goetz-Stankiewicz, *Variations of Temptation—Vaclav Havel's Politics of Language*, in *Critical Essays on Vaclav Havel*, ed. Marketa Goetz-Stankiewicz and Phyllis Carey (New York: G. K. Hall & Co, 1999), 237.

10. Burian, *Leading Creators of Twentieth-century Czech Theatre*, 185.

11. Thomas Richards, *At Work with Grotowski on Physical Actions* (New York: Routledge, 1995), 4.

12. Peter Brook, "Preface," in Jerzy Grotowski, *Towards a Poor Theatre* (New York: Simon and Schuster, 1968), 13.

13. Edwin Wilson, *The Theater Experience*, 6th ed. (New York: McGraw-Hill, 1994), 265.

14. John Keane, *Vaclav Havel: A Political Tragedy in Six Acts* (New York: Basic Books, 2000), 483–85.

15. In 2012 a second play co-written with Accettura about Czech heroes was completed and produced in the Czech Republic. *The Flights of Jan Wiener* focused on this Czech hero who fled Czechoslovakia as a young man while the Nazis moved into his country. Wiener then fought the Nazis as part of the Czech squadron of the British Royal Air Force against Hitler. *The Flights of Jan Wiener* also incorporated the language of gesture and Grotowski ideographs to represent the many obstacles faced by Wiener in his life as part of the history of the Czech people. For example, dance and movement were used to convey the suicide of his father and stepmother in his presence as they decided to die rather than be taken to a concentration camp. The actress portraying Wiener's mother did a powerful dance of somber but smoothly elegant movements, culminating with her on her back on the floor representing the death of Jan Wiener's mother in Terezín.

16. A third play co-written with Accettura about Czech heroes was performed in the Czech Republic in 2014. *The Mystery of Mucha* focuses on the life of famed Czech art nouveau artist Alphons Mucha and his son, who were good friends with Czech composer Bohuslav Martinů. When they visited the Mucha Museum in Prague, the student actors marveled at the scope of Mucha's graphic artwork, created for the theatre productions of French actress Sarah Bernhardt (another character in the play). At the museum they also saw videos and other material on Mucha's life. At the National Gallery of Art in Prague they were amazed at the scope of the huge paintings in Mucha's Slav Epic series of twenty huge paintings showing the history of the Slavic people. In addition to performing at the international theatre festival in Hradac Králové, the students later performed the play twice in the National Gallery in Prague in front of Mucha's Slav Epic paintings.

Finding Common Ground

Lessac Training across Cultures

Erica Tobolski and Deborah Kinghorn

Teaching in a culture and country other than your own requires a contradictory mix of planning and improvisation. Mastery of the subject matter is essential, but perhaps more important is sensitivity to and knowledge of the culture of the student, and an ability to problem solve, making adjustments in order to accommodate the student's cultural context and learning environment. In order to shed light on this process, we examine our individual experiences with voice training through Lessac Kinesensics in Malaysian and Croatian university classrooms. Our findings are part of a long-range research project steered by the Lessac Training and Research Institute.

One of the primary research areas of the Lessac Institute is determining the efficacy of the use of Lessac Kinesensics (LK) as theatre voice pedagogy in various first languages (L1). The Lessac Institute hypothesizes that LK can effectively be used along with theatre voice training approaches in various L1s as well as in acquisition of a second language (L2) within theatre voice training. In the case of English as a Second Language (ESL) learning, or even accent acquisition, the disconnect or conflict between the student's internalized first culture and the implicit cultural patterns of the second language creates a gap between physical impulse and the act of speech that results in lack of authenticity in behavior and in vocal expression. Lessac expert trainers Tobolski and Kinghorn have undertaken steps to show how Kinesensic body and voice training can create a psychosomatic connection that will link the actor to impulse and to her original culture, allowing her to feel "at home" when communicating in the L2.

Lessac Kinesensic Training is a holistic approach to actor training that seeks to engage the student in the development of her authentic voice. Lessac training relies on "finding new ways of stimulating the senses, much the way a child is naturally inclined to develop. Through psychosomatic learning, we teach ourselves to feel and perceive internal, physical experience and learn experientially that the sensory or feeling process is the currency through which we communicate with ourselves."[1] This learning is predicated on finding "familiar events" that "are actions performed with ease thanks to talent or skill, and are, thus, likely pleasurable, graceful, and efficient. They are a healthy use of the body."[2] These familiar events provide the bases for "organic instruction," the conscious use of the familiar event (which has been generated by the body's natural impulse) as a fundamental teaching tool. Organic instruction is "the body teaching you instead of you attempting to exert control over your body."[3]

In our economically driven global society, "English is perceived as the world's lingua franca."[4] In order to compete and succeed, the perception is that one must learn English, often at the expense of one's first language. Because culture and language are inextricably linked, to lose one's language may cause one to lose connection with one's identity. As Leveridge states: "The relationship between language and culture is deeply rooted. Language is used to maintain and convey culture and cultural ties. Different ideas stem from differing language use within one's culture and the whole intertwining of these relationships start [sic] at one's birth."[5]

How, then, does language acquisition affect actors for whom English is a second language (L2), and who are exhorted to learn to speak English because it will help them get work? In South Africa, for example, where plays are frequently performed in English so that everyone in that multilingual society can understand them, an actor without English will lose many opportunities to work. But if an actor is expected to be, above all, honest in the portrayal of character, how is truthfulness achieved when the language of execution is not the actor's first language, the language that informs her culture and her identity?

Learning to speak English by mimicking American or British broadcasts may be effective for general conversation, but for the purposes of the actor, for whom words form the vital path to imagination, remembrance, emotion, physical response, and action, mimicry is not enough. Referring to the imitation of British mannerisms, customs, and speech adopted by East Indians during the British Empire's imperialist rule, Homi Bhabha suggests mimicry can be seen as "one of the most elusive and effective strategies of colonial power and knowledge....Colonial mimicry is the desire for a reformed, recognizable Other, *as a subject of difference that is almost the same, but not quite*. Which is to say, that the discourse of mimicry is constructed around *ambivalence*; in order to be effective, mimicry must continually produce its slippage, its excess, its difference."[6] "Slippage" or "difference" speaks to an effect which is put on, like a costume, but which is not a faithful representation of the person beneath. Therefore, as Jacques Lacan states, "The effect of mimicry is camouflage....It is not a question of harmonizing with the background, but against a mottled background, of becoming mottled—exactly like the technique of camouflage practised in human warfare."[7] Here, Lacan suggests that although mimicry allows one to pass unharmed, the true person must be hidden in order to succeed. Such hiding can become denial of one's culture and one's language, which can then adversely affect one's identity, making it more difficult for the actor to access inner emotion, imagination, and response. As Lessac says, mimicry "is destructive by virtue of the fact that it influences us to accept as right only one kind of learning that…obscures our…ability to learn creatively from our own internal body environment."[8]

As the concept of mimicry implies, voice and movement teachers whose L1 is English may perceive their training methodologies to be universal, yet those methods can contain hidden assumptions of cultural superiority. Take, for example, the case of a South African woman whose L1 is Afrikaans. Asked why, when speaking English, her voice is low-pitched, even confined rigidly in that register, but when speaking Afrikaans her voice is characterized by wide range and fluidity, her response is, "That's what I was taught." By whom? "By my American teachers. I am to speak in this lower range because, for a professional woman, it is expected." When questioned further, she says, "Afrikaaner women tend to use a lot of range (many more soprano pitches) when speaking, and it is part of our culture. I don't want to restrict my voice to this lower register, but I understand that when I speak English, this is expected of me in order to succeed in this training."[9] This is an unfortunate case of diminution of a voice due to cultural overlaying, however unconscious, on the part of the instructor.

How do English-speaking teachers of voice and speech for performance navigate these troubled waters to help actors retain their cultural identities while sounding authentic in what is for them a foreign language? Perhaps the answer lies in a more holistic approach to teaching English by utilizing the L1 as the basis for learning the L2. This approach is supported by remarkable work done in South Africa utilizing translanguaging, described as "using one language to reinforce the other in order to increase understanding and in order to augment the pupil's ability in both languages."[10] To slightly rephrase Mbulungeni Madiba, "The distinguishing feature of translanguaging pedagogy is that it focuses on the [person] rather than the teacher, that is, how a learner uses the available linguistic repertoires to develop deeper understanding of the subject."[11] The result is development of the student's unique vocal identity.

According to a translanguaging approach, if an actor is to embody the L2, then the implication is that the voice and speech teacher must have an awareness of and respect for central aspects of the speaker's first language.

These include, but are not limited to, the consonant and vowel patterns of the language, the primary point of sound resonation in the sinus, the oral cavity, and the throat, and the oral shape or posture used in forming speech sounds. Likewise, knowledge of a country's history and current culture is keenly important before stepping into the classroom to teach a Western curriculum rooted in Western practice. Even then, despite prior research into a culture, there is always learning to be done *in situ*.

We each found surprises and challenges in our respective Malaysian and Croatian classrooms. At both of the universities we visited, classes are routinely taught in English. Yet students had varying levels of fluency in English and, lacking an interpreter, several students functioned as unofficial translators for their fellow classmates. Malaysia and, to only a slightly lesser extent, Croatia are hierarchical societies, and, in the case of Croatia, patriarchal, where authority figures are not questioned or challenged, particularly in a student/professor relationship. Consequently, when a question is posed, students are apt to answer affirmatively whether or not there is full comprehension. Students generally want to please their superiors and fear giving the incorrect answer. In our experiences abroad, when students were queried about their experiences following an exploration into the use of their voices or their understanding of a body movement, the instructors were greeted with slightly embarrassed smiles and silence. No one wanted to risk giving a potentially wrong answer. No doubt this was exacerbated by the fact that students encountering a Western instructor, possibly for the first time, were processing complex information in what was for them a second or even third language. The following case studies, provided by each expert trainer, help to illustrate the importance of preparation and a culturally sensitive approach to voice and movement training.

Case Study 1
Teaching and Coaching in Malaysia, by Erica Tobolski

During an eleven-month period spanning 2008–2009, I spent two semesters at the Universiti Teknologi-MARA in Shah Alam, Malaysia, as a Distinguished Visiting Professor. I taught several courses in voice/speech and acting and served as the voice and acting coach for a Malaysian language production of *A Midsummer Night's Dream*. With only a rudimentary background of the country and its customs and with my knowledge of the language at a tourist's level, I found myself on a slow learning curve in the classroom. I quickly learned the extent of what I did not know. Most notably, the so-called language barrier is not the only challenge for a teacher from a foreign country coming into a host country. Cultural differences, I soon discovered, ranged from differentiations in teacher-student roles and behaviors to a lack of common icons. It became clear that adjustments to my teaching style and pedagogical approach were necessary in order to be effective. The very tenets of Lessac Kinesensics—perception, awareness, and response—are the same strategies I used to navigate unfamiliar waters in which I was as much student as teacher.

In the months leading up to my travel to Malaysia, I undertook research into the country's history and culture. One of my goals was to adapt to the culture and avoid teaching from an imperialist viewpoint. I consulted several resources, including Craig Storti's *The Art of Crossing Cultures*, a guide for visitors to understanding the difficulties of entering another culture and strategies for integration. *Culture Shock! Malaysia*, a volume in the *Culture Shock!* series, provided practical information on behavior and customs.[12] Research into Malaysia's political and social history further fueled my desire to avoid imposing my American culture and values through my teaching.

Malaysia has a long history with both multiculturalism and colonialism. This multi-racial country is made up of Muslim Malays (50 percent), Chinese (23 percent), indigenous peoples (12 percent), and Indians (7 percent).[13] Each community practices its own language, religion, traditions, and mores. Malaysia has been ruled by many outside countries and became an independent country relatively recently, in 1957. Prior to independence, British rule lasted approximately 130 years.[14] British influence is apparent in government structure, language, and educational systems, though there is a growing movement toward nationalism and an accompanying debate on the quantity of English instruction in the schools. The government policy is one of equality. However, like most countries with racially diverse populations, Malaysia experiences conflicts between its ethnic groups. Efforts to address inequalities continue in the realms of government and education, and there is a sense that the younger generations have greater interracial harmony.[15]

Teaching and learning styles in Malaysia present some key differences from those in the United States in both practice and approach. Observation of the teaching of traditional Malaysian performance styles such as Wayang Kulit (shadow puppets) and Mak Yong (song and dance punctuated with spoken dialogue) reveal a transmissional style of learning where the student mimics the form as presented by the master teacher.[16] Emphasis is placed on copying the teacher move-for-move because the student is learning and preserving a historical art form.

Proficiencies like watching closely and following exact instructions are necessary for successful acquisition of performance skills. Additionally, Malaysia is a hierarchical society, and this dynamic tends to be present throughout teacher/student interactions, both within and outside of the classroom. Teachers are authority figures to be respected and answered rather than questioned. This is a distinct contrast to the student-centered and transactional learning styles more often utilized in the United States.[17] One of the cornerstones of higher learning in the United States is the Socratic method of critical thinking, a distinctly Western philosophy of instruction.[18]

Given these differences, I realized it was necessary for me to consider the transmissional approach. I recalled my own experiences with learning through transmission; dance choreography, playing an instrument, and singing were my own "familiar events." Recalling these experiences helped me to understand the students' expectations and find a way to introduce them to new information and new learning styles. One way to make the bridge from transmissional learning to transactional learning was to find performing events that were familiar and then introduce LK principles. Transmissionally acquired, traditional performing arts were comfortable for the students in their familiarity and structure, easing the way for new ideas. For example, a student struggled with a balancing gesture in a dance intended to replicate feeding baby birds. By using the "pleasure smelling" principle, she found ease and balance, opening the door to a transactional form of learning.[19] After achieving the necessary physical technique, she was able to add her personal images in interpreting the dance.

Imposing a philosophically divergent approach without introduction is confusing to students and counter-productive to testing the application of Lessac Kinesensics to L2. Therefore, it was necessary for me to be straightforward in my approach. The teaching and application of Lessac Kinesensics would take place in English; however, the goal was for the Malaysian students to utilize aspects of their own language and culture in order to have a deeper connection to their voices, whether they were speaking in English or Malay (also called Bahasa Malay). As described above, introducing LK through "familiar events" uses a transactional approach, where an individual employs their prior experiences and personal associations in order to understand new concepts. If the Lessac Kinesensics' explorations of voice and speech are perceived to be universal strategies, then it is necessary to find common ground through universally shared experiences.

Finding common ground initially began through musicality. Music and singing in Malaysia are essential aspects of the culture. Traditional performance forms include the gamelan orchestra as well as several distinct theatrical forms that weave song and dance with live music and the spoken word.[20] Music and singing accompany ceremonies, festivals, and worship not only among Muslim Malays, but in the Chinese and Indian communities as well. Music is a major part of both the traditional arts and popular culture. It is not uncommon to walk down the street and hear people humming or singing. It therefore made sense to use music and musical metaphors as a way for students to access LK principles.

Arthur Lessac created a metaphoric model wherein instruments of the Western orchestra are paired with the consonant sounds of English.[21] Several "sound effect" objects are also included, such as a radiator for the "s" sound and a fan for the "f" and "h" sounds. The philosophy behind this model is twofold: to develop the musicality of each speech sound's unique and expressive qualities in the speaker's voice, and to provide a familiar event in order to develop a sensory or kinesensic experience.[22] String, brass, and woodwind instruments create melodic, legato tunes, while percussive instruments punctuate the music and create staccato rhythms.

Many consonant sounds are shared between Malay and English; however, working within the Lessac Kinesensics consonant orchestra resulted in some challenges. Malaysian students were familiar with most of the sounds but not the instruments of the Western orchestra. Where possible, traditional instruments used in Malaysian performing arts and the gamelan orchestra were substituted. In regard to sound qualities, the *serunai*, a double-reed oboe, most closely resembled the sound of the Western oboe, which is paired with the "ng" (International Phonetic Alphabet symbol /ŋ/) sound (the final consonant of any word ending in "-ing"). The three-stringed *rebab* stood in for the "n" violin, and a variety of cymbals, gongs, and drums from the gamelan orchestra were comparable to the timpani drums for the "b," "d," and "g" sounds.

As with the consonants, there were particular challenges in teaching the Lessac tonal sounds of y-buzz and +y-buzz, found in the vowels of the words "see" and "say" (IPA /i/ and /eɪ/).[23] These had to do with the use of the letter "y" and the general oral shape in Malay. Every language and regional dialect within that language is influenced and created by an oral shape or posture. David Alan Stern, a dialectician who has designed programs from which to learn various dialects, talks about the "Point of Resonance," a primary location in the oral cavity where sound is directed and focused.[24] In speakers of Malay, this oral cavity shape creates a slightly hyper-nasal quality. In words with the /i/ vowel (as in "fleece"), this posture creates a challenge to achieving the y-buzz. There is no diphthong as in the word "say" (IPA /eɪ/) in Malay, eclipsing the usefulness of the +y-buzz unless one is speaking English.

According to Arthur Lessac, "Tonal energy begins when the vocal sound waves contact the body structures of the [facial] mask (nasal and cheekbones) and set them vibrating. The vibrating bony sections of the hard palate, teeth, mask and head set up direct and sympathetic vibrations that amplify vocal sounds."[25] This vibratory feeling is a beneficial relaxer-energizer and provides an optimal acoustic output without muscular strain or push. The method of achieving the quality of the y-buzz is by drawing the lips slightly forward as if to make the sound "shhh." The /y/ (IPA /j/; the French horn in LK) consonant plus the /i/ vowel (pronounced "yeee") are then introduced into the mouth shape of the "shhh" sound, resulting in a buzzy vibratory sensation in the alveolar ridge (or gum ridge). The forward facial orientation effectively lengthens the vocal tract, and this, combined with directing the vibrations to the teeth, creates a sound that can be described as a quality that is richer and warmer than the pure /i/ vowel.[26] The oral posture that creates the /i/ vowel is described by phoneticians as "close" and "front."[27] It is achieved by raising the tongue and spreading the lips into a smiling position, resulting in a sound with a perceived bright quality. This is distinctly different from the y-buzz quality of bone-conducted resonance achieved by directing the vocal vibrations to the back of the front teeth. The Lessac +y-buzz, a diphthong (IPA /eɪ/), is produced with forward-focused resonance as with the y-buzz.

Although the /i/ vowel, as in the word "see," is shared by both English and Malay, teaching the y-buzz presented a challenge for several reasons. The letter "y" is less common in Malay than in English. It is used exclusively as a consonant in Malay (rather than as either consonant or vowel in English) and consequently is of short duration. Even when the /i/ sound exists as a vowel in Malay, it tends to be of shorter duration than in English, where its duration is variable.[28] Additionally, the Lessac orchestra instrument for the "y" sound is the French horn, an instrument unfamiliar to most Malaysian students. Substituting another instrument for the French horn is necessary, the obvious choice being the *serunai*, the Malaysian oboe-like instrument that also stood in for the "ng" sound as described above. Although the "y" sound is used less often, developing the tonal current of the y-buzz was beneficial in speaking in L2 and in singing applications. This was evident when a student struggled with a challenging one-and-a-half octave jump in a traditional Mak Yong song. He found tonal resonance first by singing a popular song. This familiar event, combined with the y-buzz principle, enabled him to sing with ease and accuracy and a greater amount of tonal resonance.

Students studying theatre in Malaysia love to sing and are much less inhibited with vocalizing than their American counterparts. Consequently, the Lessac exploration of the "scat band," improvising rhythms and melodies using the consonant orchestra, came easily to the Malay students. There was no hesitation or embarrassment about making sound; rather, it was a joyous endeavor. This willingness and facility with sounds made the bridge to speaking a much easier prospect. Explorations with poems in English and in Malay were enriched with a new awareness of how sound could deepen expressiveness by simultaneously illuminating the text and the speaker's experience.

During the course of study, students learned the fundamentals of Lessac Kinesensics and applied them to movement and voice explorations. The results were evident in the presentations of poems and monologues that were performed in both English and Malay. The students demonstrated a full, embodied expression that honored the text and illuminated the speaker's personal experience. Vocal resonance and clarity of speech were evident, and movement revealed character impulses and actions. Students noted how Lessac Kinesensics supported the development of their characters in *A Midsummer Night's Dream*. The student playing the character Demetrius wrote in his final paper, "We learned a very famous technique which was 'smelling the flower.' This uses imagination and when we imagine that we're breathing in the smell of the flower, we become more relaxed and focused. The vocal vibration is the technique that I use to make my voice heard around the arena."[29] In witnessing the students' use of LK principles, I believe there was a positive impact on the students' voice in both L1 and L2. Moreover, they were more confident and focused on stage and their voices were clear and resonant.

Case Study 2
Teaching and Coaching in Croatia, by Deborah Kinghorn

From 2011 to the present, I have taught at various intervals at the University of Rijeka in Croatia at what is now known as the Academy of Arts. The longest stint there was in 2013, when I spent five months there as a Fulbright Scholar. On my initial visit in 2011, I was immediately confronted with my naiveté and colonialist assumptions. While students who were accepted into the program had to speak English, and while my job was to improve their English-speaking skills, I quickly found that my humor and idioms—the things I rely on when I teach in the United States to create a sense of bonding and familiarity—failed me. I needed to obtain more knowledge about the country and the language, including learning basic words and phrases to better understand the feel of speaking the language before returning to Croatia in 2013.

The Croats arrived in present-day Croatia sometime between the sixth and ninth centuries of the Common Era. The country has a long history of invasion and takeover by other countries. At various points in history, portions of the country were absorbed by Hungary, Italy, the Ottoman Empire, France, Austria, and Germany. The establishment of Yugoslavia only further blurred the concept of Croatian identity. During World War II, ethnic cleansing by Hitler's regime was carried out against Jews, Serbs, and Romas, and Croats were targeted by the Croatian fascist government. After the war an uneasy union between all ethnic groups was imposed by Josep Broz Tito, which included combining their languages into one amalgamation known as "Serbo-Croat-Bosnian." Not until 1991 did Croatia declare independence, resulting in further war and ethnic cleansing, which ended in 1995. Tension still remains between the Croats and the Serbs who did not leave at the end of the war. Since then, Croatia, along with Serbia and Bosnia, have actively sought to cleanse their respective languages of the influences of the others.[30]

Knowing this history illuminated for me remarks I had heard from students, such as "Our voice does not count" and "We are only a little country."[31] My students, who as children between the ages of eight and twelve had lived through the Homeland War (1991–1995), were still scarred by it—many living with recurring nightmares and daily wariness, like combat veterans with PTSD. Croatia's official language is now Croatian, spoken by nearly 96 percent of the population. It is a south Slavic language, written in the Latin alphabet, and has three major dialects. Of all L2 languages spoken in Croatia, English is the most widespread, with 49 percent of the population speaking it.[32] While my students understood the program requirement to speak English, they told me they could not feel authentic performing in the language. Rightly or wrongly, I attributed this to a new sense of national identity, which, it seemed, could be snatched away at any minute, in addition to the fact that their L2 acquisition was predominantly through mimicry of popular American television programs.

My solution to helping my students find authentic expression in English was to introduce them to the sensation of voice in the body through experimentation in breathing, alignment, and sound creation, without the overlay of accent or language. Released from the confines of *any* language, the students' voices opened up and resonated freely, their ranges increased dramatically, and their breathing was unconsciously deep and full. These abilities were achieved through the Lessac concepts of vibration as the guide for sound production (tonal energy), playfulness as the medium for expression, and "smelling the flower" as the familiar event for natural, relaxed breathing. These Lessac concepts are foundational to all voice and body expressiveness regardless of culture or language.

Using the Lessac concepts, we explored open-mouthed sounds and felt the differences that occurred when we altered the lip opening from smallest to largest. We explored how the sound changed when the jaw was at different stages of openness. We investigated obstructing the free flow of sound with the tongue and lips and enjoyed the pleasant humming that occurred. With the obstructions in place, we turned the voice on and off, like a light switch, and noted the difference in sensation and quality. We explored quick releasing of the tongue from the hard palate or gum ridge and the quick separation of the lips, noting the light staccato sounds we could make. We created rhythms and melodies as individuals, then joined together to form duets, trios, scat bands, choirs, and other forms of shared vocal expression.

During this segment of the learning process, we focused on three principles of Lessac training. The first was the Human Likeness Principle: "All human organisms, throughout the world, at one and the same time: are the same, vary, and are totally different. Although our dimensions vary, and experientially, each of us is unique, we are all structurally and organically precisely alike."[33] Therefore, in our explorations, no one and no sound could be "wrong" or favored above another, since our commonality was both being human and being individuals. Second, we used the Human Musical Instrument Principle: "The body is a remarkable musical instrument. It is a string instrument, a reed, brass, percussion and sound effect instrument. The body can be 'played upon' and 'play itself.'"[34] Our musical explorations were not composed, but they reflected the music of Croatian culture, with rhythms, tonal colorings, and expressiveness that, while foreign in some ways to me, were completely pleasurable and familiar to my students. This leads to our third principle, that of "Carefreeness." As Lessac asserts, "When we sense 'carefree' awareness, we viscerally understand how not to accommodate tension which results in the absence of tension."[35] Carefreeness was clearly felt by the students when they playfully "smelled the flower," and in their subsequent realization of the loss of tension in their core muscles that previously had inhibited and patterned their breathing.

After these explorations, our next step was to find musicality and carefreeness when speaking in Croatian. By recognizing and welcoming the familiar events of humming, tapping, and making music, we enhanced awareness of the phonemes of the Croatian language. We began with the same playful explorations of open sounds, but now identified specific Croatian language vowels, noting how different lip shapes and the relative space between the upper and lower molars altered the sound. This led us to a visceral feel of what Lessac calls "structural energy," which is described as "a kinesthetic energy state related to facial posture...revealing the existence, nature, and functioning of an unconditioned reflex of the jaw."[36] Students noted their voices felt "fuller" and "less effortful."[37] As we obstructed the free flow of tone, we explored consonants, now taking specific note of their unique properties, such as voiced and unvoiced, and tapped or sustained (hummed). We also took note of when consonants were dropped, such as prior to other consonants or at the ends of words. By feeling these formerly dropped consonants as part of the rhythm of their language, the students incorporated them more willingly into their speech than if I had insisted on "better diction." For example, in the word "blitva" (Swiss chard), the /t/ is often not executed. By tapping the /t/ lightly, students found a new rhythm that was pleasing, and which also resulted in clearer enunciation. In the phrase "dobar dan" (good day), the final /n/ in everyday speech is barely audible, yet when the students explored a brief sense of humming that sound, they also found more satisfaction in communicating the phrase (one student said, "I feel like I really mean it now")[38] as well as more clearly enunciating it. In my observations, the students experienced greater intelligibility without forsaking their own rhythms or innate dialects, and they discovered it through playing and music-making, not through imitation or mimicry.

In all our experimentation, I never insisted on a right or wrong way, but instead focused on quality of tone and ease of vocal production. By the time we were ready to turn to English, we had accomplished two important things that would make our work easier. First, the students' explorations had given them a newfound appreciation both for their voices and for the intricacies and beauty of their own spoken language. Second, they had identified means by which they could improve quality of tone and articulation without resorting to imitation of a prescribed "standard" of speech.

In order to engender a sense of ownership for the Croatian students when speaking the English language, we began with the same playful explorations of voice and speech. However, this time we focused on noting the differences in sensation between the two languages while also exploring points of commonality. For example, we found that the students' /o/ vowel had all the desirable characteristics needed for good tone, but that in order to sound more English or American, the vowel needed a smaller, rounder lip opening. This shift could be felt muscularly (through structural energy) and was therefore easy to achieve and retain. That same /o/ in Croatian had the approximate lip opening for /ɔ/ (an open mid-back rounded vowel, as in "brought" or "call") or /ɒ/ (open back rounded vowel, as in "hot" or "rock") in English, and became a touchstone for finding that sensation whenever they encountered those vowels. Through the pleasurable process of discovery and experimentation, the students found themselves learning an English/American accent, based on sensory knowledge of their own language. Simultaneously, we were able to adhere to the pronunciation characteristics of both English and Croatian.

The results of our work were evident when the students performed their final scenes in both Croatian and English. The element that had been missing—ownership of the language—was now fully present, for *both* languages. The students' voices were resonant, their physical actions fully embodied, and their performances confident and truthful. Lessac Kinesensic's familiar event and organic instruction created the conditions wherein the students could find common ground between the two cultures and their respective languages, thus increasing their ability to feel "at home" in a second language.

Conclusion

As our experiences in Malaysia and Croatia show, there is much more to teaching English than pronunciation of words, but the words we speak are deeply connected with our identities and with our cultures. Voice and speech teachers would do well to remember that identity is deeply connected with language and that we need to honor sociolinguistic paradigms while facilitating optimal vocal health. Fluency in an L2 will manifest itself when the student finds a way to make the language part of her identity. According to our experiences, it will occur sooner if the pathway to learning utilizes familiar events from the L1, which provide the necessary basis for self-instruction without mimicry. Lessac Kinesensics identifies those familiar events, strengthens the student's awareness of them in the L1, and then utilizes them as organic instruction for the acquisition of the L2, forming an organic bridge between the two.

These two case studies demonstrate that by seeking elements of vocal production that are universal and by fully engaging students in embodying sound of all kinds, we can use the culture and language of origin to help us teach a second language. In doing so, we empower our students with the familiar sensations and sounds of their own language, even as they speak a foreign one, which forms the link between impulse and action that is missing in imitation-driven language acquisition models.

Notes

1. Arthur Lessac, *Body Wisdom: The Use and Training of the Human Body* (New York: Drama Book Specialists, 1981), 20.

2. Arthur Lessac and Deborah Kinghorn, *Essential Lessac: Honoring the Familiar in Body, Mind, Spirit* (New York: RMJ Donald, 2014), 11.

3. Ibid., 13.

4. T. Kim, *Shifting Patterns of Transnational Academic Mobility: A Comparative and Historical Approach* (London: Comparative Education, 2009) 45 (3): 387–403.

5. Aubrey Neil Leveridge, "The Relationship between Language & Culture and the Implications for Language Teaching," TEFL.net, http://edition.tefl.net/articles/teacher-technique/language-culture/, accessed May 4, 2016.

6. Homi Bhabha, *The Location of Culture* (New York: Routledge Classics, 2004), 122.

7. Jacques Lacan, "The Line and the Light," in *The Four Fundamental Concepts of Psychoanalysis*, trans. Alan Sheridan (London: Hogarth Press and the Institute of Psycho-Analysis, 1977), 99, quoted in Bhabha, *Location of Culture*, 121.

8. Lessac, *Body Wisdom*, 16.

9. Private interview, name withheld, January 2013.

10. C. Williams, *A Language Gained: A Study of Language Immersion at 11–16 Years of Age* (Bangor: University of Wales School of Education). https://www.bangor.ac.uk/addysg/publications/Language_Gained.pdf, accessed April 15, 2016.

11. Mbulungeni Madiba, "Promoting Concept Literacy through Multilingual Glossaries: A Translanguaging Approach," in *Multilingual Universities in South Africa: Reflecting Society in Higher Education*, ed. Liesel Hibbert and Christa van der Walt (Bristol: Multilingual Matters, 2014), 74.

12. Heidi Munan, *Culture Shock! Malaysia* (Singapore: Marshall Cavendish International [Asia] Pte Ltd, 2005).

13. "Population of the World," http://www.livepopulation.com/country/malaysia.html, accessed September 6, 2016.

14. "The Commonwealth, Malaysia: History," http://thecommonwealth.org/our-member-countries/malaysia/history, accessed May 14, 2016.

15. "Many Ethnicities, Many Cultures, One Nation: The Malaysian Experience," http://www.academia.edu/1113674/Many_ethnicities_many_cultures_one_nation_the_Malaysian_experience, accessed September 6, 2016.

16. "European University Institute, Teaching and Learning," http://www.eui.eu/ProgrammesAndFellowships/AcademicCareersObservatory/CareerTips/TeachingLearning.aspx, last updated July 30, 2015.

17. Transactional theory insists that the reader's individuality must be respected and considered, and that readers initially understand a work only on the basis of prior experience. They cannot make sense of a text except by seeing it in the light of other experiences, other texts. The reader's background, the feelings, memories, and associations called forth by the reading, are not only relevant, but are the foundation upon which understanding of a text is built. And so transactional theory invites the reader to reflect upon what she brings to any reading, and to acknowledge and examine the responses it evokes. R. E. Probst, "Transactional Theory in the Teaching of Literature," (Urbana, Ill.: ERIC Clearinghouse on Reading and Communication Skills, 1987), http://www.ericdigests.org/pre-926/theory.htm.

18. R. Paul and L. Elder, "The Commonwealth: Socratic Teaching," Foundation for Critical Thinking, 1987, http://www.criticalthinking.org/pages/socratic-teaching/606, last accessed on May 14, 2016.

19. Pleasure smelling, or "smelling the flower," is an essential "Familiar Event"

of LK that encourages the body's natural way of expansive breathing through qualitative rather than quantitative means. Lessac and Kinghorn, *Essential Lessac*, 11–12.

20. Prof. Dr. Ghulam-Sarwar Yousof, ed., *The Encyclopedia of the Malaysia: Performing Arts* (Singapore: Archipelago Press, 2004). The gamelan orchestra or ensemble has its roots in Indonesia. It is made up of various sizes of metal gongs, bronze-keyed instruments, barrel drums, and xylophones. These instruments, along with violin-like stringed instruments and oboe-like instruments are grouped in various configurations for traditional performing art forms of Joget, Menora, and Mak Yong, where stylized dance, music, and dialogue are interwoven. These folk theatre forms have roots in ancient Thai and Malay shamanism, ritual beliefs, and myths and may incorporate contemporary and topical news as well as clown characters similar to those in commedia dell'arte.

21. Arthur Lessac, *The Use and Training of the Human Voice* (Mountain View, Calif.: Mayfield, 1997), 70.

22. Ibid., 6–7.

23. For more on y-buzz and +y-buzz, see http://www.vasta.org/newsletter-past/02/2002spring.pdf, last accessed February 19, 2017.

24. Dr. David Alan Stern, "Dialect Accent Specialists, Q and A about Accent Reduction," https://www.dialectaccentspecialists.com/store/index.php, accessed May 14, 2016.

25. Lessac, *Use and Training*, 124.

26. Marth Munro, Timo Leino, and Daan Wissing, "Lessac's Y-Buzz as a Pedagogical Tool in the Teaching of the Projection of an Actor's Voice," *South African Journal of Linguistics* 34 (December 1996): 25–36, in *Collective Writings on the Lessac Voice and Body Work, A Festschrift*, ed. Munro, Leino, and Wissing (Ft. Lauderdale, Fl.: Llumina Press, 2009), 327–39.

27. *Handbook of the International Phonetic Association* (Cambridge: Cambridge University Press, 1999).

28. Christopher Byrnes and Tam Lye Suan, *Teach Yourself Malay* (Chicago: McGraw-Hill, 2006).

29. Student paper, name withheld, April 2009.

30. "Croatia," https://www.britannica.com/place/Croatia, last modified May 31, 2016.

31. In-class conversation with students, March 2013.

32. "Croatia."

33. Lessac, *Body Wisdom*, 5.

34. Ibid.

35. Ibid., 6.

36. Ibid., 57.

37. In-class conversation, April 2013.

38. Ibid.

Contributors

Becky K. Becker, *Theatre Symposium* editor, is Interim Executive Director for the Center for International Education and Professor of Theatre at Columbus State University in Columbus, Georgia. She serves on the Publications Committee for the Southeastern Theatre Conference and is currently the Vice Chair of the National Playwriting Program for Region 4 of the Kennedy Center American College Theatre Festival. In addition to directing regularly, her research includes cross-cultural theatre and communication, new plays, and embodied cognition. She has published in *Review: The Journal of Dramaturgy, Theatre Symposium, Feminist Teacher, Theatre Journal*, and various edited volumes.

Karen Berman is Chair of Theatre and Dance at Georgia College. Her work in high-impact, engaged learning has resulted in interdisciplinary collaborative classes in theatre for social change involving community-based theatre with at-risk youth. She has taken students to perform three times in the Czech Republic. She was elected into the prestigious College of Fellows of the American Theatre, where she currently serves as dean. Berman is a past president of the Association for Theatre in Higher Education and co-founder of Washington Women in Theatre. She holds a PhD from Capella University and an MFA from Catholic University and has directed over 100 plays.

Chase Bringardner is an Associate Professor of Theatre at Auburn University in Auburn, Alabama. He received his PhD and MA degrees in Theatre History and Criticism with an emphasis in Performance as Public Practice from the University of Texas at Austin. He has published in *Theatre Topics, Theatre Journal*, and *Performing Arts Resources*, and has a chapter in *The Oxford Handbook of the American Musical*. His current research projects include a manuscript on regional identity in musical theatre as evidenced through the "Southern" musical as well as a sociocultural performance history of the Fabulous Fox Theatre in Atlanta, Georgia.

Daniel Ciba is a PhD Candidate in Drama at Tufts University. He received his MA in Theatre from Villanova University in 2012, where he served as dramaturg for Marina Carr's *Woman and Scarecrow*. He has presented at a variety of venues, including the Philadelphia Theatre Research Symposium, the SETC Theatre Symposium, the Association for Theatre in Higher Education, and the Humanities Education and Research Association Conference. His current research explores the intersections of memory theory and queer performance, using performance histories of Tennessee Williams's plays. His work has been published in *Praxis* and *Theatre Research International*.

Anita Gonzalez is Professor of Theater and Drama at the University of Michigan, where she leads the Global Theatre and Ethnic Studies minor. Her research interest is in the area of intercultural performance, particularly the ways performance reveals histories and identities in the Americas and in transnational contexts. Her books include *Black Performance Theory* (2014), a coedited anthology with Tommy DeFrantz; *Afro-Mexico: Dancing between Myth and Reality* (2010); and *Jarocho's Soul: Cultural Identity and Afro-Mexican Dance* (2004). Other publications include articles about intersections between theatre and dance ("Negotiating Theatrics: Dialogues of the Working Man," *The Oxford Handbook of Dance and Theater*, 2015), maritime culture ("Megaship Economies and Transnational Maritime Performance," *Theatre Research International*, 2014), utopia in Urban Bush Women performance (*Modern Drama*, 2004), archetypes of African identity in Central America ("Mambo and the Maya," *Dance Research Journal*, 2004), and the pedagogy of teaching African American drama (*Theatre Topics*, 2009). She was a founding member of the Urban Bush Women, has choreographed for Ballet Hispanico, taught theatre in Central America and the United Kingdom, given professional and educational workshops in Caribbean and African American dance, and lectured about new play development. She has authored plays and musicals, including *Liverpool Trading – New York* (with Richard Aellen), *Le Hot Blu* (with composer and writer Ken Lauber), and *Ybor City* (with composer Dan Furman). Recent directing projects include *Sun and Shadows*, a Guatemalan shadow puppet play; *DARASA*, a civil rights musical by Lorna Littleway; and *Nobody*, a play about Bert Williams and George Walker by Richard Aellen (2011). She earned her PhD in Theater and Performance Studies from the University of Wisconsin–Madison (1997). She is an executive board member of the National Theatre Conference, an associate member of Stage Directors and Choreographers, and a member of the Dramatists Guild, the Association for Theatre in Higher Education, the American Society for Theatre Research, and the Society of Dance

History Scholars. Dr. Gonzalez currently serves as a member of the executive committee of the University of Michigan Press.

Deborah Kinghorn is Master Teacher of Lessac Kinesensic Voice and Body Training and Professor and Director of Acting at the University of New Hampshire. She has served as voice, text, and dialects coach for over 100 productions in many theatres, and has presented and taught in Croatia, South Africa, Brazil, England, and Finland. She is a member of "Power Play," an interactive applied theatre group, and co-author of *Essential Lessac: Honoring the Familiar Body, Spirit, Mind*. A recipient of two teaching awards as well as the Leadership Award from the Lessac Training and Research Institute, she is also a member of the Voice and Speech Trainers Association and past president of the Louisiana Tech Research Institute.

Sarah McCarroll, associate editor of *Theatre Symposium*, is an Associate Professor of Theatre at Georgia Southern University. In addition to courses in theatre history and script analysis, she teaches costume design and is the costume shop supervisor. Her research interests include costume history, the historical body, late nineteenth-century British theatre, and cognitive embodiment. Sarah's work may be found in *Theatre Symposium 23: Theatre and Youth* as well as in the anthology *Languages, Bodies, and Ecologies: Theatre, Performance and Cognition*. For the past decade, her professional home has been the Utah Shakespeare Festival, where she has been a dramaturg, first hand, and wardrobe supervisor.

Sunny Stalter-Pace is an Associate Professor of English at Auburn University. Her first monograph, *Underground Movements: Modern Culture on the New York City Subway*, was published by University of Massachusetts Press in 2013. She has published articles on modern drama in the *Journal of American Drama and Theater* as well as in *Transfers: Interdisciplinary Journal of Mobility Studies*. Her current book project is titled *Gertrude Hoffmann: Imitation Modernist*, a study of Hoffmann's long career as a comedienne, dancer, producer, and choreographer to reframe current scholarly conversations about modernist aesthetics. Her other research interests include mobility in/and modern drama, nostalgic performance, and musical theatre.

Erica Tobolski is an Associate Professor in Theatre at the University of South Carolina and was a Fellow for the Center for Teaching Excellence there in 2011 and 2014. In 2008–2009 she was a Distinguished Visiting Professor at Universiti Teknologi in Malaysia. She has coached voice, text, and dialects for the Utah Shakespeare Festival, the Great River Shakespeare Festival, Charlotte Repertory Theatre, the Lost Colony, the Clarence Brown Theatre, and Istana Budaya (Malaysia), among others, and also for the film *The Wise Kids*. Her work has been published in *The Complete Voice and Speech Workout* and *The Voice and Speech Review*.

E. Bert Wallace is an Associate Professor of Theatre at Campbell University, where he teaches theatre history, playwriting, and directing; directs plays; and oversees both the Drama and Christian Ministry and the University Honors Programs. He earned his MFA in Playwriting/Dramaturgy from the University of Alabama. His work has been published in *Theatre Symposium* as well as in *Christianity and Theatre* and *Southern Theatre*. His most recent playwriting project, an adaptation of Paul Green's novel *This Body the Earth*, was produced in April 2016 in cooperation with the Paul Green Foundation. Research interests include the history and interactions of Christianity and theatre and Spanish colonial theatre practice in Puerto Rico.